IN MEMORIAM

JUDGE PATRICK DAVID CURRAN QC

1948 – 2021

Faithful to Christ; loving to family;
loyal to friends

quia erat vir bonus,
et plenus Spiritu Sancto, et fide.

A Lawyer's Translation from the Original Greek

Malcolm Bishop QC, MA (Oxon)

Bencher of the Inner Temple; a former deputy High Court Judge and Recorder; Hon. Fellow and Hon. Standing Counsel, Regent's Park College, Oxford University

With an introduction by Dr Brendan Devitt

Saint Matthew's Gospel

A Lawyer's Translation from the Original Greek

Malcolm Bishop QC

Matador
9 Priory Business Park,
Wistow Road, Kibworth Beauchamp,
Leicestershire. LE8 0RX
Tel: 0116 279 2299
Email: books@troubador.co.uk
Web: www.troubador.co.uk/matador
Twitter: @matadorbooks

ISBN 978 1800463 295

British Library Cataloguing in Publication Data.
A catalogue record for this book is available from the British Library.

Printed and bound by CPI Group (UK) Ltd, Croydon, CR0 4YY
Typeset in 11pt Century Gothic by Troubador Publishing Ltd, Leicester, UK

Matador is an imprint of Troubador Publishing Ltd

Dedicated to the Christian Martyrs of the Middle East and Africa

And behold I am always with you,
to the very end of the age!
(Matthew 28:20)

Aid to the
Church in Need
ACN UNITED KINGDOM

FOUNDATION
FOR RELIEF AND
RECONCILIATION
IN THE MIDDLE EAST

www.acnuk.org
Tel: 02086 428668

www.frrme.org
Tel: 01730 267673

All profits will be donated for the relief of the
suffering church in the Middle East & Africa.

About This Book

Following the warm reception of my translations of the Gospel of Saint John, Saint Mark and the Book of Revelation, I have been further emboldened to attempt a translation of the Gospel according to Saint Matthew. My aim continues to be that of using my lifelong experience in the use of words as a barrister and Q.C. to inform my translation. As in the above volumes, I have preserved the use of the "present tense" in the original Greek, even though in English we might have expected a "past tense." The reason Matthew often uses the present tense, interspersed with the past (sometimes in the same sentence!), is to create a vivid, lively narrative, that brings the story of Jesus to life. Initially, it may sound strange to the reader's ear (for e.g. when we read, "he says," instead of, "he said,"), but as one gets familiar with Matthew's use of the present tense it should become less odd sounding. On a personal note, I have relished the sense of urgency and immediacy that this stylistic quirk brings to dialogues and narratives in Matthew. It is unfortunate that contemporary bible translations do not register its significance.

About the Translator

Malcolm Bishop QC is a prominent British barrister and Queen's Counsel. He has practiced throughout England and Wales at every level as well in the Caribbean. Before studying Law at Oxford University he read Theology where he learned Biblical Greek as part of his Honour Moderations. Throughout his legal career he has read his Greek New Testament for comfort and inspiration. He has recently revised his Greek knowledge under the supervision of Dr Brendan Devitt, himself an accomplished Greek scholar. His translation of Saint John's Gospel, the Book of Revelation and Saint Mark's Gospel, (also published by Matador), has been well received. He now offers this new translation of Saint Matthew's Gospel from the perspective of a practising lawyer.

Thanks

I owe my Greek teachers over the years an enormous debt of gratitude: the late Mr Warner, senior classics master at Ruabon Grammar School for guiding me through my first faltering steps in classical Greek; the Rev. Aubrey Argyle for teaching me grammatical rigour at Oxford; and especially Dr Brendan Devitt* who not only took me painstakingly through a Greek revision course but also fired my enthusiasm to attempt my translations of the books of the New Testament, a work in progress. My thanks are also due innumerable legal colleagues who have over the years honed my attempts to be clear and succinct in my written work, as well as for their lively discussions on matters spiritual while awaiting a jury's verdict. However, I take sole responsibility for any errors or oversights. It is, I believe, propitious that I send this work to the publishers on the feast day of Saint Richard Gwyn, martyred for his Catholic faith in my boyhood town of Wrexham on 15th October 1584. Let his dying words, in Welsh— "Iesu, trugarha wrthyf" ("Jesus, have mercy on me"), be ours in these troubled times.

As ever, I greatly welcome all comments: malcolmbishop@3harecourt.com

17th October 2020
The Feast Day of Richard Gwyn
Saint and Martyr

*Dr Devitt is a graduate of Dublin and Oxford Universities and teaches New Testament Greek and Biblical Hebrew to students, all over the world via Skype. He can be contacted at: drbwd301@gmail.com

Introduction

The opening line of an old English nursery rhyme (sometimes referred to as the "Black Paternoster") preserves for us the order in which the gospels have come down to us: *Matthew, Mark, Luke and John/Bless the bed that I lie on.* Matthew's primacy reflects the stature and esteem in which the book was held in the early Church; it also reflects the belief (popular until the eighteenth century) that Matthew was the first gospel to be written, and therefore the most authoritative. A gospel that bore the name of one of Jesus's twelve apostles was naturally a highly prized possession. Matthew had been personally called by Jesus to be a disciple, had sat at his feet when he taught both publicly and privately, and had seen him perform miracles throughout his ministry. He was also among the first of Jesus's followers to be sent out on a mission to "the lost sheep of the house of Israel." More significantly, Matthew had been witness to Jesus's death and resurrection, and is listed in the Acts of the Apostles as being among those awaiting the coming of the Holy Spirit at Pentecost. In this light Matthew's gospel would have been perceived as having superior authority than the writings of Mark, and the gentile physician, Luke, neither of whom belonged to Jesus's original core of twelve apostles. (Even the gospel of John, traditionally believed to have been written by a disciple who was even closer to Jesus than Matthew, does not seem to have usurped Matthew's primacy— perhaps because the latter was indeed the first to be written, as the Greek Church Father, Papias of Hierapolis [*fl.*60-150AD], suggests). However, when all four gospels were composed, copied, distributed among the various Christian communities, and later read and commented upon by theologians and bible scholars, it was evident that each of the evangelists had a particular and unique take on Jesus's life. Each emphasised different aspects and truths about his mission and identity. Mark lays stress on Jesus's powerful words and deeds, as Son of God; Luke (along with his companion volume, Acts), highlights how the message of salvation that was first preached in rural Galilee spread as far as Rome, the imperial capital. John, by contrast, takes us on more of an inner, mystical journey, that affords us glimpses and insights into Jesus's divine life, rooted in his relationship with his heavenly Father, and expressed in and through his flesh and blood existence as a human being.

Matthew's gospel also touches on many of these themes, but draws especial attention to Jesus's Jewish roots: in particular his attitude towards Jewish beliefs and traditions, religious leaders, the synagogue and temple cult, as well as with the prophetic writings, which Matthew claims Jesus brought to fulfilment in his life, death and resurrection. There are sound reasons for believing that Matthew wrote his gospel in some measure as a riposte to Jewish antagonism against Christians, possibly in Jerusalem, or groups further afield, in places such as Antioch or Rome, where diaspora Jews would have encountered Christians proclaiming the good news of Christ for the first time. We see this tension, in particular, in Matthew's account of Jesus's denunciation of the Jewish leaders as hypocrites, and in Matthew's claim that the priestly establishment in Jerusalem made up lies about the disciples stealing Jesus's body. At Jesus's trial moreover Matthew reports that the Jews cried out, "his blood be upon us," which implies a collective rejection of Jesus (though at another level it may reflect Matthew's desire that this cry might eventually become a genuine plea for atonement and salvation). For these, and other reasons, it has been suggested (notably since the holocaust) that Matthew's gospel has "anti-Semitic" tendencies. Through the centuries, it is maintained, Christian antipathy towards Jews, in the shape of racism, pogroms, expulsions, murders and executions, were inspired by the kind of words that Matthew put in the mouth of Jesus. Thus as the Jews hated Christ, it is posited, so Christians responded in kind. While we must accept that Christians have periodically adopted murderous and hostile attitudes towards Jews, it is wrong to suggest that Matthew's gospel is culpable in this regard. Matthew, like Jesus, was himself a Jew. He wrote as Jew, interpreted scripture as a Jew, and like all Jews held out hope that someday God's Messiah would come to redeem and deliver Israel from its enemies. It was just that Matthew conceived that these promises had been realised in the person of Jesus of Nazareth. That Matthew believed Jewish hopes and expectations had come to a climax in Jesus did not imply the annulment of Judaism, so much as its fulfilment. Some theologians and biblical scholars however continue to accuse Matthew of being "supercessionist," meaning that Matthew thought that the coming of Christ rendered Judaism a defunct religion. This, however, is surely incorrect. As a Jew, Matthew wanted his fellow Jews and co-religionists to recognise in Jesus the climax of all that the prophets had spoken about regarding Israel's salvation. That Matthew highlights, among other things, the tension and conflict between Jesus and the religious establishment, only serves to show the nature of the "in-house" debate that was going on within the Jewish community regarding the status of Jesus. Matthew belonged to and was part of the Jewish community that had to grapple with the implications of Jesus's career. He can hardly be called "anti-Semitic" for weighing in on the debate, or even for criticising or disagreeing with his co-religionists. As a Jew, Matthew believed that he had a strong case for arguing that Jesus was in fact God's long awaited Messiah. He is concerned that his fellow Jews will miss out on God's blessing if they ignore the gospel proclaimed by Jesus. So he set out to prove to his fellow Jews, and perhaps also to show interested Gentile converts, that Jesus is God's chosen one, the saviour and redeemer of Israel—and also of the wider world. He sets out to prove this in a number of ways, predominantly by viewing Jesus's life and ministry through the lens of the Hebrew scriptures. If Jesus is the Messiah, Matthews suggests, then there will be scriptural evidence to back up this claim. It should be possible, in other words, to see the promises of redemption and salvation in the bible outworked or fulfilled in the person of Christ. So at the very start of his gospel Matthew compiles a genealogy that traces Jesus's ancestry back to Abraham via king David, through whose lineage the

Messiah was expected to come. He points out, for example, that Isaiah foretold that a saviour would be born of a virgin and would be known as Immanuel, "God with us." In the rest of his gospel Matthew shows how Jesus mediated, or more precisely, became God's presence among his people. At the close of his gospel, in the very last verse, Matthew underscores this point by informing his readers that God, through the person of his Messiah, would always be among his people, even till the end of time. God would no more be separate from them, because he had definitively redeemed them through the Messiah's sacrificial death.

Matthew explores this notion further by highlighting how in his life, death and resurrection, Jesus took upon himself the role of historic Israel, by undergoing the same experiences that it went through in its journey with God. Thus when Joseph and Mary return from exile in Egypt, after fleeing king Herod, Matthew says that a prophecy in Hosea was fulfilled which states, "Out of Israel I called my son." Although in the first instance this refers to historic Israel, fleeing pharaoh in Egypt, Matthew sees it as having a deeper significance in pointing to the call of Jesus to serve God as his viceroy or emissary. Whereas Israel largely failed in this mission, Matthew contends that Jesus succeeded. Hence when Jesus is tempted in the desert by Satan for forty days, he triumphs in the very arena where Israel failed during its forty-year moral and spiritual examination in the wilderness. For Matthew, Jesus is the obedient Son of God, living selflessly and obediently in ways that pleased God, in contrast with the disobedient and rebellious children of Israel. But for Matthew, Jesus is also the new Moses. In three lengthy chapters detailing Christ's Sermon on the Mount, a Moses-like Jesus proclaims the values and ethics of God's kingdom. Here we encounter a radical reinterpretation of the Jewish Torah in which Jesus transcends strict or literal observances of Mosaic Law, to make explicit the underlying principle of love that should really be animating our relationships with God and other people. So whereas adultery was legally defined as having sexual relations with somebody else's wife or husband, Jesus would argue that this particular sin is committed at a much earlier stage, at the point where one begins to look lustfully at another person. Likewise, says Jesus, everybody will be familiar with the commandment that prohibits murder; but if our hearts burn with anger towards another individual then, according to Jesus, we are as guilty as if we had we killed them. Jesus also warns how easily religious ritual, which is meant to focus our attention on God, can become a bind and suffocate us with its shallowness and superficiality, such that we imagine our rote prayers impress God, because they are long, drawn out. The Law also permits us to seek redress when others violate our rights. Moses speaks of "an eye for an eye, and a tooth for a tooth." But Jesus says, if anybody takes advantage of you, turn the other cheek, go out of your way to do them good, instead of seeking compensation. In each case Jesus elevates his interpretation of scripture above that of the fathers, and even the literal text of scripture itself: "You have heard that it was said...but I say to you." Nothing could be more challenging and confrontational than for Jesus to suggest that his own word carries greater weight than Mosaic Law. Yet Jesus also said that he had not come to "abolish the Law and the prophets, but to fulfil them." If then his attitude towards the Judaism of his day seems to be one of iconoclasm, it was only insofar as he sought to rescue people buried beneath layers of man made rules and traditions. This, of course, was nothing less than the prophets did, and the reason why so many people thought that Jesus himself was a prophet, in the style of an Elijah or Jeremiah.

But Matthew's Jewish Jesus is more than just a prophet. Symbolically, he reconstitutes the twelve tribes of Israel in the guise of his twelve apostles (a sure sign that God's promised kingdom was finally at hand), and sends them out to preach the gospel to Israel. Here he fulfils Isaiah's prophecy that Messiah would give sight to the blind, cleanse lepers, raise the dead and preach good news to the poor. Matthew identifies Jesus as God's chosen servant, an important figure in the second half of the book of Isaiah. Often referred to as the "suffering servant," this individual is sometimes linked with Israel in its capacity as God's witness or representative, but more intriguingly with a messianic figure who is destined to rule the nations—but not before he suffers at the hands of his own people, for whom also he dies as an atonement for their sins. In his account of the last supper, Matthew interprets this sacrificial death as the sealing of a "covenant" (or "new covenant," in some manuscripts), symbolised by bread and wine (Christ's "body" and "blood"). Yet Matthew's emphasis on God's "chosen servant" also concerns his role in bringing "justice" to the Gentiles, and in causing them to "hope" in God's "name"—something that was not on the agenda of the Jewish authorities, who, in the spirit of Ezra and Nehemiah, sought to separate themselves from the uncircumcised.

This sheds light on later chapters, where several of Jesus's parables spell out the judgment that awaits Israel and it's spiritual leaders. In the parable about the tenants, Jesus warns that those who were entrusted with the task of producing a harvest from the vine, will suffer the death penalty for abusing servants, and later for murdering the son of the vineyard owner, all of whom were sent to gather fruit. Thus Jesus warns that the vineyard will be let out to others (i.e. the Gentiles) who, by contrast, will produce fruit in its season. To emphasise the precarious position of the Jews, Matthew writes two substantial chapters in which Jesus decries the failed spiritual leadership and hypocrisy of the scribes and Pharisees, and also that of the priestly establishment, whose temple, Jesus predicts, faces complete annihilation as judgment from God. This underscores Matthew's wider concern to show that the old way of accessing and worshipping God is coming to an end. In his passion narrative he speaks of the curtain of the temple (i.e. the holy of holies) being rent in two, symbolising that everybody, through the Messiah's death, could enter God's presence. There was no further need therefore for the high priest to enter the sanctuary (once a year), to offer atonement for sins, either for his own, or for those of the people. Coupled with Jesus's prediction about the destruction of the temple, Matthew affirms what he had earlier said about the Gentiles receiving "justice" and "hope." For Jesus was now the locus of God's presence. In his life, death and resurrected life, he had become, and had shown himself to be,

"God with us." At the close of the gospel, Jesus commands his followers to make disciples of "all nations, baptising them in the name of the Father, and of the Son, and of the Holy Spirit." Thus the gospel that starts out with a highly Jewish-centred understanding of Christ and his mission ends, with an apostolic commission to bring the good news about the saviour to the pagan, Gentile world. It is significant then that Jesus admonishes his followers to teach the nations "all that *I* have commanded you." It is not Mosaic Law or temple rituals that the Gentiles must observe, but the Law of Love, which Christ preached in his Sermon on the Mount.

Dr Brendan Devitt

Chapter One

The Genealogy of Jesus Messiah vv 1–17

The book of the genealogy of Jesus Messiah, the son of David, the son of Abraham: Abraham fathered Isaac, and Isaac fathered Jacob, and Jacob fathered Judah and his brothers, and Judah fathered Perez and Zerah by Tamar, and Perez fathered Hezron, and Hezron fathered Ram, and Ram fathered Amminadab, and Amminadab fathered Nahshon, and Nahshon fathered Salmon, and Salmon fathered Boaz by Rahab, and Boaz fathered Obed by Ruth, and Obed fathered Jesse, and Jesse fathered David, the king. And David fathered Solomon by Uriah's wife, and Solomon fathered Rehoboam, and Rehoboam fathered Abijah, and Abijah fathered Asa, and Asa fathered Jehoshaphat, and Jehoshaphat fathered Joram, and Joram fathered Uzziah, and Uzziah fathered Jotham, and Jotham fathered Ahaz, and Ahaz fathered Hezekiah, and Hezekiah fathered Manasseh, and Manasseh fathered Amos, and Amos fathered Josiah, and Josiah fathered Jechoniah and his brothers, at the time of the exile to Babylon. After the exile to Babylon Jechoniah fathered Shealtiel, and Shealtiel fathered Zerubbabel, and Zerubbabel fathered Abiud, and Abiud fathered Eliakim, and Eliakim fathered Azor, and Azor fathered Zadok, and Zadok fathered Achim, and Achim fathered Eliud, and Eliud fathered Eleazar, and Eleazar fathered Matthan, and Matthan fathered Jacob, and Jacob fathered Joseph, Mary's husband, of whom Jesus was born, who is called Messiah. Therefore all the generations from Abraham to David were fourteen generations, and from David to the exile to Babylon fourteen generations, and from the exile to Babylon to the Messiah fourteen generations.

Joseph obeys the angel vv18–25

This is the account of how the birth of Jesus the Messiah came about. Mary, his mother, was engaged to be married to Joseph, but before they came together she was found to be pregnant by the Holy Spirit. But because her husband, Joseph, was a just man and did not want to disgrace her publically, he planned to divorce her discretely. But as he was thinking about this, behold an angel of the Lord appeared to him in a dream, saying, Joseph, son of David, don't be afraid to accept Mary as your wife, because what is conceived in her is from the Holy Spirit. She will give birth to a son, and you shall name him Jesus, because he will save his people from their sins. All this took place to fulfil what the Lord had said through the prophet, **Behold, the virgin will conceive and give birth to a son. They will call him Immanuel, which means, God with us.** When Joseph woke up he did what the angel of the Lord had told him, and took Mary as his wife, but he did not consummate the marriage until she had given birth to a son, whom he called Jesus.

Chapter Two

Following the birth of Jesus in Bethlehem, Judaea, during the reign of King Herod, there came astrologers from the East to Jerusalem, saying, Where is the one born king of the Jews? We saw his star at its rising, and have come to worship him. When King Herod heard this he was gravely concerned, as was all Jerusalem. So he summoned together the chief priests and legal experts, and asked them where the Messiah should be born. In Bethlehem, Judaea, they told him. For this is what the prophet wrote: **And you, Bethlehem, in the land of Judah, you are by no means least among Judah's princes, for a ruler will emerge from you who will shepherd my people, Israel.** Then Herod invited the astrologers to meet him secretly, and he found out from them the precise time that the star appeared. Then he despatched them to

Bethlehem, saying, When you get there, search for the child with utmost care. When you've found him, let me know so that I too can come and worship him. So the astrologers listened to what the king had to say and went on their way to Bethlehem. And the star, which they had seen in the East, went in front of them until it eventually stood over the place where the child was. When they saw the star they were ecstatic with joy, and having entered the house they saw the child with Mary his mother, so fell to their knees and worshipped him. Then they opened their treasure boxes and presented him with gifts—gold, incense and myrrh. Then after being warned in a dream not to return to Herod, they returned to their homeland by a different route.

Refugees in Egypt vv13—18

After they had left, an angel of the Lord appeared to Joseph in a dream and said, Up you get and take the child and his mother and escape to Egypt, and stay there until I tell you. So Joseph got up and taking the child and his mother with him by night, he left for Egypt where he remained until Herod's death. This fulfilled the Lord's word through the mouth of Jeremiah the prophet: **Out of Egypt I called my**

son. When Herod realised that the astrologers had tricked him he was beside himself with fury. He sent and killed all of the male children aged two and under in Bethlehem and the surrounding area. He based this on calculations he received from the astrologers. This fulfilled Jeremiah's prediction: ***In Ramah a voice was heard, weeping and great lamentation, Rachel weeping for her children. And she would not take comfort, because they were no more.***

The exiles return to Nazareth vv19—23

But when Herod died, behold an angel of the Lord came in a dream to Joseph in Egypt. Get up, he said, take the child and his mother and go to the land of Israel, for those who were seeking the child's life are dead. So up he got and took the child and his mother, and went to the land of Israel. But when he heard that Archelaus was reigning over Judaea in place of his father Herod, he was afraid to go there, and after being warned in a dream he left for the region of Galilee. So he went and lived in a city called Nazareth, so that what the prophets had foretold might come to pass: ***He shall be called a Nazarene.***

Chapter Three

The Baptist proclaims his mission vv 1—12

At that time John the Baptist comes preaching in the Judean desert, saying, Repent, for the Kingdom of heaven is at hand. For this is the one that was spoken about by Isaiah the prophet, saying, **A voice of one shouting in the desert, Make ready the way of the Lord, make straight paths for him.** John wore clothes of camel's hair with a leather belt around his waist, and his food was locusts and wild honey. So people began flocking to him from Jerusalem and all Judaea, and the whole region around the Jordan. And they were being baptised by him, in the Jordan confessing their sins. But when he saw many of the Pharisees and Sadducees coming to be baptised by him he said to them, You brood of vipers! Who warned you about the coming wrath? Bear fruit that shows you've repented. And don't presume to say to yourselves, We've

Abraham as our Father. For I say this to you, God's able to raise up children to Abraham from these stones. Already the axe is at the root of the trees, and every tree that doesn't produce good fruit will be cut down and thrown into the fire. I baptise you with water for repentance, but the one who succeeds me is more powerful than I am—I'm unworthy to carry his sandals. He'll baptise you with the Holy Spirit and with fire. His winnowing fork is in his hand, and he'll clean out the threshing floor. He'll gather the wheat into the barn and will burn up the chaff with unquenchable fire.

The baptism of Jesus Messiah vv13—17

Then Jesus comes from Galilee to the Jordan to be baptised by John. But John was trying to dissuade him, I need to be baptised by you and yet you come to me! Jesus replied, Let it be so for now—it's only fitting that we should fulfil all righteousness. So John relented. And when Jesus was baptised, immediately after he came out of the water, the heavens were opened and he saw the Spirit of God coming down on him like a dove. And a voice from heaven said, This is my well-loved Son—I take great delight in him.

Chapter Four

Jesus tempted in the desert vv1–11

Then Jesus was led by the Spirit into the desert to be tempted by the devil. When he had fasted forty days and forty nights he was hungry. And the tempter came and said to him, If you're the Son of God, order these stones to become bread. He replied, It's written: **Man can't live by bread only, but by every word that comes out of God's mouth.** Then the devil brings him to the holy city and stood him on the pinnacle of the temple and says to him, If you're the Son of God throw yourself down, because it's written, **He will order his angels concerning you, and they will carry you in their hands, in case you dash your foot against a stone.** Jesus said, Again it's written: **You shall not test the Lord your God.** So again the devil takes him to a very high mountain and shows him all the earth's kingdoms and their glory. And he said to him, I'll give you all this if you fall down and worship me. Be off with you Satan, says Jesus, for it's written: **You shall worship the Lord your God and serve only him.** Then the devil leaves him, and suddenly angels came and began to serve him.

Jesus starts his ministry vv12–17

When Jesus heard that John had been arrested he went off to Galilee. Then after he left Nazareth he went to live in Capernaum by the sea, in the district of Zebulun and Naphtali. This was in order that the message spoken through the prophet Isaiah might be fulfilled: **Land of Zebulun and land of Naphtali—the coastal route, beyond the Jordan, Galilee of the Gentiles. The people sitting in darkness have seen a great light, and on those living in the region and shadow of death, light has dawned on them.** From then on Jesus began to preach, saying, Repent for the kingdom of heaven is near!

The first disciples called vv18–22

As he was strolling by the Sea of Galilee, he spotted two brothers, Simon (known as Peter) and his brother Andrew, casting a net into the sea, for they were fishermen. So he says to them, Come, follow me, and I'll make you fish for men. Instantly they left their nets and followed him. And moving on he saw two other brothers, James, Zebedee's son and his brother John, they were mending their nets in the boat with their father Zebedee, and he called them. Straightaway they quit the boat, and their father, and followed him.

Preaching to a large crowd vv23–25

So he was going all over Galilee, teaching in their synagogues, and proclaiming the good news of the kingdom, and healing people with every kind of disease and illness. And his fame spread throughout all Syria. And they brought to him all who were sick with a variety of diseases and pains, including those oppressed by demons, as well as epileptics and paralytics—and he healed them. And great crowds followed him from Galilee and the Decapolis, from Jerusalem, Judaea and from the other side of the Jordan.

Chapter Five

Blessings from a mountain top vv1–12

When he saw the crowds, Jesus went up the mountainside, and when he had sat down his disciples came to him and he began to teach them. Happy are those who own their spiritual poverty—for the kingdom of heaven is theirs. Happy are those who mourn—they'll be comforted. Happy are the humble—for the earth will be given to them. Happy are those hungry and thirsty for justice—they'll receive it in full measure. Happy are those who show mercy—mercy will be shown to them. Happy are those pure in thought—they'll see God. Happy are the peace brokers—for they'll be known as God's children. Happy are those who suffer persecution in the cause of what is right—the kingdom of heaven is theirs. Happy are you when others insult and persecute you and say all sorts of bad things against you falsely, because of me. Be happy and rejoice! You'll have a great reward in heaven! Remember, they persecuted the prophets who preceded you in exactly the same way.

The salt of the earth vv13–16

You're the earth's salt; but if it loses its taste how will its saltiness be restored? It's now good for nothing, except to be thrown away and trampled under foot by people. You're the world's light. A city built on a hill cannot be hidden. Nor does anyone light a lamp and cover it up, but rather puts it on a stand and it lightens everything in the house. Let your light shine in this way before everybody, so that they may see the good you do and praise your Father in heaven.

Jesus Messiah fulfils the law vv17–20

Don't think that I've come to abolish the law and the prophets. I've not come to abolish them, but to fulfil them. I'm telling you the truth: until heaven and earth are gone, not one dot or dash will disappear from the law until everything's accomplished. Therefore anyone who undermines the least of these commandments, and teaches others to do the same, will be called the least in the kingdom of heaven. But whoever practices and teaches them, will be regarded as great in the kingdom of heaven. For I tell you, unless you surpass the Pharisees and the legal experts in righteousness, you'll never enter the kingdom of heaven.

Teaching about murder vv21–26

You've heard what was said to people long ago, **Don't murder**, and anyone who commits murder is liable to judgment. But what I say is this: anyone who's angry with his brother will be subject to judgment. And whoever says to his brother, You idiot, will be subject to the court, and whoever says, You fool, will be at risk of hell fire. So if then you're in the process of bringing your gift to the altar and remember that your brother has a grudge against you—leave your gift before the altar and first go and be reconciled with your brother, and then come back and offer your gift. Settle matters quickly with your opponent, while you're going to court with him, lest your opponent deliver you to the judge, and the judge to the guard, and you be flung into prison. Truly I tell you, you won't get out of there until you've paid the last penny.

Teaching about sexual wrongdoing vv27–30

You've heard that it was said to the men of old, **Don't commit adultery.** But I tell you whoever looks at a woman lustfully has already committed adultery with her in his heart. So if your right eye causes you to sin, gouge it out and throw it away—it's better for you to lose one part of your body, than to have your whole body thrown into hell. And if your right hand makes you sin, cut it off and throw it away, it's better to lose one body part than for your whole body to be cast into hell.

Teaching about divorce vv31—32

It's been said, **Anyone who divorces his wife must give her a certificate of divorce.** But I tell you, anyone who divorces his wife, except for sexual immorality, makes her an adulteress. And anyone who marries a divorced woman commits adultery.

Teaching about oaths vv33—37

And you've heard said to people long ago, **Don't break your oath, but perform the vows**

you've made to the Lord. But I tell you, don't swear at all, either by heaven, for it's God's throne, or by the earth, for it's his footstool for his feet—or by Jerusalem, for it's the city of the Great King. Nor should you swear by your head, for you can't make a single hair white or black. All you need to say is a simple, Yes or No. Anything more comes from the evil one.

Teaching about revenge vv38–42

You've heard it said, **Eye for eye, tooth for tooth;** but I say, don't resist an evil person. If anyone slaps you on the right cheek, turn your other cheek to him too. And if anyone wants to sue you and take your shirt, hand over your coat as well. And if anyone forces you to go one mile, then go two miles with him. Give to the person who asks you, and don't turn down the person who wants to borrow from you.

Teaching about love vv43–48

You've heard it said, **Love your neighbour** and hate your enemy. But I say, love your enemies, pray for those who persecute you. In this way you'll be sons of your Father in heaven. For he makes his sun to shine on both the evil and the good, and sends rain on the just and the unjust. If you love only those who love you, what good is that? Don't tax collectors do the same? And if you only greet your relatives, what more are you doing than others? Even pagans do that—don't they? Be perfect therefore, just as your Father in heaven is perfect.

Chapter Six

Giving to the poor vv1—4

Don't make a show of your piety in front of others, for then you'll have no reward from your Father in heaven. So whenever you give to the poor don't announce it with the blast of a trumpet, as the hypocrites do—in the synagogues and in the streets—in order to be praised by others. In truth, they have their reward in full. But when you give to the poor don't let your left hand know what your right hand's doing, so that your giving will be in secret. Then your Father who sees in secret will reward you.

Teaching about prayer vv5—15

And whenever you pray don't be like the hypocrites. They love to pray standing in the synagogues and at street corners to be seen by all. Truly I tell you, they have their reward. But when you pray go into your room, shut the door and pray to your Father who is hidden. Then your Father, who sees in secret, will reward you. And when you pray don't keep on babbling like pagans—they think they'll be heard because they use lots of words. Don't be like them, your Father knows what you need before you ask him. Pray then like this: Our Father in heaven— all honour to your name! May your kingdom come. May your will be done on earth, as in heaven. Give us our food for today. Forgive our wrongdoing, just as we've forgiven those who've wronged us. Don't lead us into trials that overpower us, but deliver us from the evil one. For if you forgive those who wrong you, then your heavenly Father will also forgive you. But if you don't forgive others their wrongdoings your Father won't forgive you your sins.

Fasting vv16–18

Whenever you fast don't be like the long-faced hypocrites. They disfigure their countenance so others can tell that they're fasting. Seriously, I tell you, they've had their reward. But when you fast, spruce up your appearance—scrub your face so that others can't tell that you're fasting, except your Father who is hidden. And your Father, who sees in secret, will reward you.

Possessions vv19–24

Don't stockpile riches on earth where moths and worms devour, and where thieves break in and steal. But store up for yourselves treasures in heaven, where neither moths nor worms destroy and where thieves don't break in and steal. For wherever your treasure is, that's where your heart will be. The lamp of the body is the eye. If your eyes are healthy your whole body will be radiant with light; but if your eye is evil your whole body will be plunged into darkness—and what a darkness that will be! Nobody can serve two masters. He'll either hate one and love the other, or he'll be devoted to one and despise the other. You can't serve God and money.

No need to worry vv25–34

So I tell you, don't worry about your life—what to eat or drink, or about your body, what you will wear. Isn't life more important than food or the body more than clothing? Look at the birds of the air, they don't sow, reap or gather into barns, and yet your heavenly Father feeds them. Aren't you much more valuable than they? And which one of you can, by worrying, add a single inch to his height? And why do you worry about clothing? Think about the lilies in the fields, how they grow. They don't work or spin, and yet not even Solomon in all his splendour clothed himself like one of these. So if that's the way God clothes the grass in the fields, which is here today and tomorrow thrown onto the fire, won't he much more clothe you—O you with little faith! Stop worrying, saying, What shall we eat? What shall we drink? What shall we wear? The Gentiles are obsessed with such things. But your heavenly Father knows that you need them all. So, first seek God's kingdom and his righteousness, and all these things will be given to you. Stop worrying about tomorrow—tomorrow will have its own worries. Today has enough trouble of its own.

Chapter Seven

Judging others vv 1—6

Don't judge, or you'll be judged. For as you judge, so you too will be judged—measure for measure. And why do you look at the speck in your brother's eye, but overlook the plank in your own? And how can you say to your brother, Let me take out the speck from your eye when there's a plank in your own? Hypocrite! First take out the plank in your own eye, and then you'll be able to see clearly to take out the speck in your brother's eye. Don't give what's holy to dogs, or throw your pearls in front of pigs, or they'll trample them under their feet, and turn on you and tear you to pieces.

Just ask vv7—12

Ask, and it'll be given to you; seek, and you'll find; knock, and it'll be opened to you. For all who ask receive, and whoever seeks finds, and for everyone who knocks it'll be opened. Which of you will give his son a stone if he asks for bread, or a snake if he asks for fish? If you then, though evil, know how to give good gifts to your children, how much more will your Father in heaven give good gifts to those who ask him? So in everything you do, treat others as you would have them treat you; this sums up the Law and the Prophets.

The wide and narrow gate vv13—14

Go in through the narrow gate. For the way is broad and the road wide that leads to destruction, and many are entering through it. So too the gate is narrow and the route is difficult that leads to life—and few find it.

Prophets true and false vv15–20

Watch out for false prophets: they come to you dressed as sheep but inwardly are ravenous wolves. You'll recognise them by their fruits. Do people pick grapes from thorn bushes or figs from thistles? So every healthy tree bears good fruit, but the unhealthy tree can't bear good fruit. Every tree that doesn't bear good fruit is cut down and thrown into the fire. So you'll know them by their fruits.

Discipleship vv21–28

Not everyone who says to me, Lord, Lord, will enter the kingdom of heaven, but he who does my heavenly Father's will. On that day many will say to me, Lord, we prophesied in your name, didn't we? And didn't we drive out demons in your name, and in your name perform many mighty deeds? Then I will tell them plainly, I never knew you—be gone, evildoers! So everyone who hears my words and puts them into practice is like the wise man that built his house upon rock. When it rained and the waters rose and the winds blew and lashed that house, it didn't collapse because it was built on rock. But everyone who hears my words but does not act on them is like the foolish man who built his house on sand and when it rained, and the waters rose, and the winds blew and beat against that house, it collapsed with a great crash. And when Jesus finished speaking the crowd was amazed at his teaching, because he taught them with authority, not like their scribes.

Chapter Eight

A healed leaper vv1–4

As he came down from the mountain large crowds followed him. And behold a leper came up to him, and falls before him, saying, Lord, if you want to you can make me clean. Jesus reached out his hand and touched him, saying, I do want to—be clean! Immediately his leprosy was cleansed. Jesus says to him, Be sure you tell no one, but go and show yourself to the priest, and offer the gift Moses commanded as evidence for them.

A centurion's faith vv5–13

When Jesus entered Capernaum a centurion came up to him, pleading with him and saying, Lord, my servant is at home lying paralyzed and suffering great anguish. Jesus says, I'll come and heal him. The centurion said, Lord, I'm not worthy that you should come under my roof. Just speak a word and my servant will be cured. For I myself am a man under authority, with soldiers under me. So I can say to this one, Go! and he goes; and to that one, Come! and he comes. And I say to my slave, Do this, and he does it.

When Jesus heard this he was astonished and said to those following him, Really—I'm telling you—I haven't found such faith, not even in Israel! I tell you this; many will come from the East and West and take their place at the table with Abraham, Isaac and Jacob in the kingdom of heaven. But the heirs of the kingdom will be hurled into outer darkness, where there'll be weeping and gnashing of teeth. Then Jesus said to the centurion, Go! As you believe so will it happen for you. And instantly his servant recovered.

Jesus heals many vv14–17

When Jesus entered Peter's house he saw his mother in law lying ill with a fever. He touched her hand and straightaway the fever left her and she got up and began to serve him. That evening they brought to him many who were demon-possessed, and with a word he cast out the spirits and healed all the sick. This was done to fulfil the word of Isaiah the prophet, who said: *He took our illnesses and bore our diseases.*

The cost of discipleship vv18–22

And when Jesus saw the crowd around him, he gave instructions to cross to the other side. A legal expert approached and said to him, Teacher, I will follow you wherever you go. Jesus says to him, Foxes have holes and the birds of the air nests, but the Son of Man has nowhere to rest his head. Another of his disciples said to him, Lord, let me go and bury my father first. Jesus says to him, Follow me, leave the dead to bury their own dead.

A storm calmed vv23–27

And when Jesus got into the boat his disciples followed him. Suddenly a great storm arose on the sea, so that the boat began to be flooded by the waves—but he was asleep. And they went and woke him saying, Save us, Lord, we're drowning! And he says to them, Why are you such cowards, men of little faith? Then he got up and rebuked the winds and the sea, and a great calm prevailed. And the men were astonished saying, What sort of person is this? Even the winds and sea obey him.

Demons expelled vv28–34

When he came to the other side, into the region of the Gadarenes, two men who were demon possessed met him as they came out of the tombs. They were so violent that nobody could pass that way. And the demons cried out saying, What have you to do with us, Son of God? Have you come here to torment us before the time? Now some pigs were feeding some distance away. The demons were begging him saying, If you're going to expel us, send us into the herd of pigs. So he said to them, Go! So they came out and entered into the pigs, and behold the whole herd rushed down the steep bank into the sea, and perished in the waters. The herdsmen fled into the city and there told everything, especially what had happened to the demon possessed men. And behold, the entire city came out to meet Jesus and they implored him to get out of their region.

Chapter Nine

Healing and forgiveness vv1—8

Jesus then got into a boat and crossed to the other side and came to his own town. And behold they were bringing to him a paralyzed man lying on a stretcher. When Jesus saw their faith he said to the paralytic, Be brave, son, your sins are forgiven! At this some of the lawyers said among themselves, This man is blaspheming. Jesus, knowing their thoughts, said, Why do you have evil thoughts in your hearts? What's easier to say, Your sins are forgiven, or, Stand up and walk? But so that you may know that the Son of Man has power on earth to forgive sins (he says to the cripple), Up you get! Take your stretcher, and go to your home. So up he got and went to his home. When the crowds saw this they were awestruck, and glorified God who had given such authority to men.

Matthew called to discipleship vv9–13

And when Jesus passed on from there, he saw a man called Matthew, sitting at the tax office, and he says to him, Follow me! So he got up and followed him. Later, when Jesus was sitting at table in Matthew's house, behold many tax collectors and sinners came and were sitting with Jesus and his disciples. When the Pharisees saw this they began to say to his disciples, Why does your teacher eat with tax collectors and sinners? When he heard this he said, The healthy don't need a doctor, only the sick. Go and learn the meaning of this, **It's mercy I want, not sacrifice**. For I haven't come to call the righteous, but sinners.

Teaching about fasting vv14–17

Then John's disciples come to him, saying, Why do we and the Pharisees fast but your disciples don't? Can the wedding guests mourn, asked Jesus, as long as the bridegroom is with them? There'll be a time when the bridegroom is taken from them, then they'll fast. Nobody puts a new patch on old clothing, because the patch comes away from the garment and it becomes worse than before. So also new wine is not put into old wineskins. If it is, the skins burst and the wine's spilled and the skins are ruined. New wine goes into fresh skins, to preserve them both.

A dead girl raised, a sick woman healed vv18–26

As he was saying all this, behold, a ruler came and knelt before him saying, My daughter's just died; but come and lay your hands on her and she'll live. Jesus got up, and together with his disciples, followed the man. And behold a woman who had suffered for twelve years with a haemorrhage came up behind him and touched the fringe of his robe, for she kept telling herself, If I only touch the fringe of his garment I'll be cured. Jesus turned around and said to her, Have courage, daughter, your faith has cured you! At that very moment the woman was healed. And when Jesus came to the ruler's house, and saw the flute players and the crowd making a commotion, he said, Be off with you! The girl's not dead, only sleeping. And they laughed at him. When the crowd had been sent away he went in and took the girl by the hand and she got up. And news of this swept through that whole region.

Two blind men healed vv27—31

And as Jesus passed on from there two blind men followed him, crying out and saying, Have mercy on us, Son of David! And when he had come to the house the blind men came to him and Jesus says to them, Do you believe that I'm able to do this? They say to him, Yes, Lord. Then he touched their eyes saying, Because of your faith—so be it! And their eyes were opened. And Jesus sternly warned them, Make sure you don't tell anybody. And after they had left they spread the news throughout the region.

A mute man healed vv32-34

As they were heading off, behold, they brought a mute man to him who was demon possessed. Once the demon had been cast out, the mute man began to speak, and the crowds were dumbstruck. Never, they said, have we seen the likes in Israel. But the Pharisees said, By the ruler of demons he is casting out demons.

Harvest and labourers vv35-38

And Jesus went around all the cities and villages, teaching in their synagogues and proclaiming the gospel of the kingdom of God, and healing all and every illness and frailty. And when he saw the crowds he was filled with compassion for them, because they were hassled and destitute, like sheep without a shepherd. Then he says to his disciples, The harvest is great, but the labourers are few. Ask therefore the Lord of the harvest to send out workers into his harvest.

Chapter Ten

The Twelve called and sent out vv1–15

Jesus called his twelve disciples and gave them authority to drive out unclean spirits and to cure every disease and illness. The names of the twelve apostles are as follows: Simon, known as Peter, and his brother Andrew; James, Zebedee's son and his brother John; Philip and Bartholomew; Thomas, and Matthew the tax collector; James, Alpheus's son; and Thaddeus, Simon the Zealot, and Judas Iscariot, who betrayed him. These twelve Jesus sent out after he had commanded them, saying, Avoid Gentile areas, don't set foot in any Samaritan town, but go to the lost sheep of the house of Israel. As you go, proclaim this message, The kingdom of heaven is near! Heal the sick, raise the dead, cleanse lepers, drive out demons. You've received freely, so give freely. Don't take gold, silver, or copper in your money belts—no bag for your journey, or two tunics or spare sandals or a walking stick—for the worker deserves his keep. Whatever town or village you come to, seek out someone who's trustworthy and stay there until you leave. As you enter the house give it your greeting, and if the house is worthy let your peace rest upon it. But if it's unworthy, take back your peace. If someone won't welcome you or listen to what you have to say, shake the dust off your feet as you leave that town. I'm telling you, it'll be more tolerable for Sodom and Gomorrah on judgment day than for that town.

Warnings vv16–42

Behold, I'm sending you like sheep among wolves. So be as wise as serpents and as innocent as doves. Watch out! People will hand you over to the courts and flog you in their synagogues. And you'll be brought before governors and kings on my account, to give testimony to them and to the Gentiles. Don't worry about what to say, or how to say it, for what you're to say will be given to you then. For it won't be you speaking, but your Father speaking through you. Brother will hand over brother to death, and a father his child, and children will rise up against their parents and have them put to death.

Everyone will hate you because of my name. But whoever's faithful to the end will be saved. If they persecute you in one town, flee to another. For the truth is, you won't complete a journey through the towns of Israel before the Son of Man comes. A student is not above his teacher; nor a servant above his master. It's enough that students become like their teachers and servants like their masters. If they've called the head of the house Beelzebub, how much more the members of his household! So don't be afraid of them; for there's nothing hidden that won't be revealed, or concealed that won't be disclosed. What I tell you in the darkness, proclaim in the light. And what you hear whispered to you, shout from the rooftops. Don't fear those who can kill the body but can't kill the soul. But rather fear the one who can destroy both body and soul in hell! Aren't two sparrows sold for a penny? And yet not one of them will fall to the ground without your Father's consent! For even the hairs of your head are numbered. So don't be afraid, you're worth much more than many sparrows! Therefore whoever will acknowledge me before men, I'll also acknowledge before my Father in heaven. But whoever disowns me before others, I'll disown him before my Father in heaven. Don't think I've come to bring peace on earth; I've not come to bring peace, but a sword. I've come to turn **a man against his father,** *a daughter against her mother, a daughter-in-law against her mother-in-law, and a man's enemies will be from his own household.* Anyone who loves their father or mother more than me is unworthy of me; anyone who loves their son or daughter more than me is unworthy of me. And anyone who doesn't take his cross and follow me is unworthy of me. Whoever saves his life will lose it; whoever loses his life because of me will find it. Whoever receives you receives me. And whoever receives me, receives the one who sent me. Whoever welcomes a prophet, because he's a prophet, will receive a prophet's reward, and whoever welcomes a good person, because he's a good person, will receive a good person's reward. And whoever gives the most insignificant of my followers a cup of cold water, because he's my follower, I assure you he won't miss out on a reward.

Chapter Eleven

The Baptist's questions answered vv1–6

After Jesus had finished instructing his disciples, he went on from there to teach and to preach in all their towns. Meanwhile, in prison, John heard about what the Messiah was doing, and sent his disciples to ask, Are you the one who's to come, or should we look for someone else? Jesus answered, Go, tell John what you hear and see: the blind receive sight, the crippled walk, lepers are cleansed, the deaf hear, the dead are raised, and the poor are brought good news— and happy is the one who isn't offended by me.

Nobody greater than John the Baptist vv7–19

As John's disciples left, Jesus began to speak about him to the crowds. What did you go into the desert to look at? A reed shaken by the wind? What did you go out to see, a man dressed in expensive clothes? No! You'll find those who wear flashy clothing in kings' palaces. So what did you go out to see? A prophet? Yes indeed, and much more than a prophet. This is the one about whom it's written, **Behold, I send my messenger ahead of you. He will prepare your way before you.** Truly, I tell you, no one born of a woman is greater than John the Baptist; yet the least in the kingdom of heaven is greater than he. From the time of John the Baptist until now the kingdom of heaven has endured violence, and violent persons are taking it by force. For all the prophets and the law prophesied until John. And if you're willing to accept it, he's Elijah who is to come. You've got ears—so listen up! To what shall I compare this generation? They're like children sitting in the market place shouting to their friends, We played the flute for you but you didn't dance; we sang a lament but you didn't mourn. For John came neither eating or drinking and they say, He's got a demon. The Son of Man came eating and drinking and they say, Look at him! A glutton and a drunkard, a friend of tax collectors and sinners! But wisdom's vindicated by its deeds.

Judgment on unrepentant towns vv20–24

Then Jesus began to denounce the towns in which his mighty deeds had been done, because they did not repent. Woe to you Chorazin! Woe to you Bethsaida! For if the mighty works which were performed among you were done in Tyre and Sidon, they would've repented ages ago, in sackcloth and ashes. Nevertheless, I tell you it'll be more bearable for Tyre and Sidon on judgment day than for you. And as for you, Capernaum, will you be exalted to heaven? No! You'll be flung down to Hades. For if the mighty works you experienced had been done in Sodom, it would've remained until now. Nevertheless, I say to you it'll be more bearable for Sodom on judgment day than for you.

The prayer of Jesus Messiah to his Father vv25–30

At that moment Jesus said, I praise you Father, Lord of heaven and earth, because you've hidden these matters from the wise and clever and revealed them to little children. Yes, Father, for this is what you were only too pleased to do. My Father's handed everything over to me. Nobody knows the Son except the Father, and nobody knows the Father except the Son, and to whomever the Son chooses to reveal him. Come to me, all you who are weary and burdened, and I'll give you rest. Take my yoke upon you and learn from me, for I'm gentle and humble of heart, and you'll find rest for your souls, for my yoke's easy and my burden's light.

Chapter Twelve

Questions about the sabbath vv 1–8

At that time Jesus walked though the grain fields on the sabbath. His disciples were hungry and began to pluck some of the heads of grain and eat them. But when the Pharisees saw this they said to him, Look, your disciples are breaking the sabbath. He answered them, Haven't you read what David and his companions did when they were hungry? He entered the house of God and ate the consecrated bread that was unlawful for him to eat (and those that were with him), but only the priests? Or haven't you read in the law that on the sabbath the priests in the temple break the law and yet are guiltless? I tell you, something greater than the temple is here! But if you'd known what this means, **I want mercy not sacrifice**, you wouldn't have condemned the guiltless. For the Son of Man is Lord of the sabbath.

Jesus heals on the sabbath vv9–14

So leaving that place he entered their synagogue, and behold there was a man there with a withered hand. And they asked him, saying, Is it lawful to heal on the sabbath? They said this to accuse him. He said to them, Who among you if he'd only one sheep and it should fall into a pit on the Sabbath, wouldn't grab it and pull it out? How much more valuable is a man than a sheep! So it's lawful to do good on the sabbath. Then he says to the man, Stretch out your hand. He did so, and it was restored, as sound as the other one. But the Pharisees went out and plotted how they might destroy him.

A prophecy fulfilled vv15–21

But Jesus knew this, and so he withdrew from there. And a large crowd followed him, and he healed all of them. But he sternly warned them that they should not make him known. He did this to fulfil what the prophet Isaiah had written: **Here is my servant, the one I have chosen, my beloved in whom my soul delights. I will bestow my Spirit upon him. And he will proclaim justice to the nations. He will not bicker nor cry out, nor will anyone hear his voice in the streets. He**

will neither break a bruised reed nor snuff out a smouldering wick, until through triumph he brings justice. And the nations will put their hope in his name.

Demons and Pharisees vv22–32

Then a blind and dumb demoniac was brought to him, and he healed him so that the mute could both speak and see. All the people were amazed, and they were saying, Could this be David's son? But when the Pharisees got wind of this they said, This man only casts out demons through Beelzebub, the ruler of demons! But knowing their thoughts he said to them, Every kingdom divided against itself is brought to ruin, and every town or house divided against itself will not stand. If Satan drives out Satan, he is divided against himself, so how then will his kingdom endure? But if it's through Beelzebub that I drive out demons, by whom do your sons drive them out? Therefore they'll be your judges. But if it's by God's Spirit that I cast out demons, then the kingdom of God has come upon you. Or how can anyone go into a strong man's house and steal his belongings unless he first ties up the strong man? Then he can ransack his house. You are either for me or against me. And whoever doesn't gather with me, scatters. So I tell you, every sin and blasphemy of people will be forgiven; but blasphemy of the Spirit won't be forgiven. So also whoever speaks a word against the Son of Man will be forgiven. But whoever speaks against the Holy Spirit won't be forgiven, either in this age or the age to come.

Rebuking the faithless vv33–37

Either make the tree good and its fruit good; or make the tree bad and its fruit bad—for from its fruit a tree is known. You brood of snakes! How can you speak good things when you're evil? For the mouth speaks what's in the depths of the heart. A good person, out of his good treasure brings out good things, but a wicked person brings out of his treasure evil things. And I tell you; on the Day of Judgment people will give account of every careless word they speak. For by your words you will be justified, or by your words you will be condemned.

Jonah's experience vv38–42

Then some of the Pharisees and lawyers answered him, and said, Teacher, we'd like to see a sign from you. He said to them, An evil and adulterous generation seeks a sign. But it won't be given a sign, except the sign of the prophet Jonah. For just as Jonah spent three days and three nights in the belly of the great fish, so the Son of Man will be three days and three nights in the bowels of the earth. The men of Nineveh will be raised at the judgment with this generation, and condemn it—because they repented at Jonah's preaching. And behold something greater than Jonah is here. The queen of the South will be raised in the judgment with this generation and condemn it; for she came from the ends of the earth to hear the wisdom of Solomon, and behold something greater than Solomon is here.

Evil spirits itinerary vv43–45

When the unclean spirit has left a person it wanders through waterless places looking for rest, but doesn't find any. Then it says, I'll return to the house I came from. And when it arrives to find the house empty, swept and put in order, it goes and fetches seven other spirits more evil than itself, and they go in and live there, and the condition of the person becomes worse than it was at first. So it'll be with this evil generation.

Jesus's family go looking for him vv46–50

As he was still speaking to the people, suddenly his mother and brothers were stood outside, asking to speak to him. But he replied to the one who had given him the message, Who is my mother? And who are my brothers? And he stretched out his hand towards his disciples, and said, Here's my mother and my brothers! Whoever does the will of my Father in heaven is my brother and sister and mother.

Chapter Thirteen

The parable of the sower vv1–9

That same day Jesus went out of the house and sat beside the sea. And great crowds gathered around him, so that he got into a boat and sat down. And the whole crowd were stood on the beach. And behold, he told them many things using parables, saying, A sower went out to sow. And as he sowed, some seeds fell along the path, and the birds came and devoured them. Other seeds fell on rocky ground, where there wasn't a lot of soil, and they sprang up straightaway, because they'd no depth of soil, but when the sun rose they were scorched, and because they'd no root they withered away. Other seeds fell among thorns, and the thorns grew up and choked them. Other seeds fell on good ground and produced grain, some a hundredfold, some sixty and some thirty. You've got ears—use them!

Then the disciples approached him and asked, Why speak to them in parables? He answered, The mysteries of the kingdom of heaven have been given to you, not to them. For to whoever has even more will be given to him, and he will have abundance. But the one who doesn't have anything, even what he has will be taken away from him. That's the reason I speak to them in parables, because seeing they don't see, and hearing they neither hear nor understand. For them the prophecy of Isaiah is fulfilled that says: **You will indeed see but never comprehend, see but never discern. Because this people's heart has become dull and they can barely hear with their ears, and they have closed their eyes, lest they should see with their eyes, hear with their ears, understand with their heart, and turn and I would heal them.** But your eyes are blessed, because they see, and your ears, because they hear. For in truth, I tell you, many prophets and righteous persons yearned to see what you see, and to hear what you hear, but didn't hear it.

The meaning of the parable of the sower
vv18–23

Listen, this is what the parable of the sower means. When anyone hears the word of the kingdom, but doesn't understand it, the evil one comes and snatches away what has been sown in his heart. That's what's been sown along the path. As for what was sown on rocky ground, that's someone who hears the word and immediately accepts it joyfully, but he's rootless and so he lasts for a little while, and when there's hardship and persecution because of the word, immediately he falls away. As for what was sown among thorns; this is the one who hears the word, but frets about worldly concerns, so that the lure of wealth chokes the word and it becomes fruitless. As for the one sown on good soil, this is the one who both hears and understands the word. So then he bears fruit and yields a hundredfold, or sixty or thirty.

The parable of the weeds and wheat vv24–30

He put another parable to them, saying, The kingdom of heaven is like someone who sowed good seed in his field. But when everyone was asleep, his enemy came and sowed weeds among the wheat, and left. When the plants sprang up and bore grain, so did the weeds. The owner's servants came and said to him, Sir, didn't you sow good seed in your field? So why has it got weeds? And he said to them, An enemy has done this. Then the servants say to him, Do you want us to go and gather them up? No, he says, in case when you gather the weeds you also uproot the wheat with them. Let both grow together until the harvest. When harvest comes I'll tell the harvesters, First gather the weeds; tie them in bundles to be burned; then gather my wheat and put it into my barn.

Parables about mustard seeds and leaven
vv31—33

He then told another parable. The kingdom of heaven is like a mustard seed that a man sowed in his field. It's the smallest of all seeds, but when it's grown it's bigger than all the plants of the garden, and becomes a tree, so allowing the birds of the air to nest in its branches. He spoke yet another parable to them. The kingdom of heaven resembles leaven that a woman took and hid in three measures of flour, until it was all leavened.

Jesus said all this to the crowds by means of parables, and told them nothing except in a parable, so that what the prophet had said might be fulfilled, saying, ***I will open my mouth in parables. I will proclaim what has been kept secret from the foundation of the world.*** Then he left the crowds and went indoors. His disciples approached him saying, Explain to us the parable of the weeds in the field. He answered, saying, The person who sows the good seed is the Son of Man, and the field is the world, and the good seed, the sons of the kingdom, and the weeds are the sons of the evil one, and the enemy who sowed them is the devil, and the harvest represents the end of the age, and the harvesters are the angels. So just as the weeds are gathered and burned in the fire, so it'll be at the end of the age. The Son of Man will send his angels, and they will weed out of his kingdom everything which causes sin, and all who do evil. They will throw them into the blazing furnace, where there will be weeping and gnashing of teeth. Then the righteous will shine like the sun in the kingdom of their Father. You've got ears—use them!

Parables of hidden treasure and a pearl vv44–46

The kingdom of heaven resembles treasure hidden in a field, that a man found and hid. Then with joy he goes and sells all he has and buys that field. Again, the kingdom resembles a merchant looking for fine pearls. When he found one of great value, he went and sold all that he had and bought it.

The parable of the net vv47–50

Again, the kingdom of heaven is like a net thrown into the sea that collected all kinds of fish. When full, men dragged it ashore and sat down, and sorted the good into containers and threw out the bad. That's what it will be like at the end of the age. The angels will come and separate the evil from the righteous, and throw them into the blazing furnace. There there will be weeping and gnashing of teeth.

These parables explained vv51–52

Have you understood all this, he asked? We have, they replied. So you see, he said to them, every scribe who has been trained for the kingdom of heaven is like a master of a house, who brings out from his treasure both old and new.

Jesus rejected at Nazareth vv53–58

Once he had finished these parables, Jesus left. When he came to his hometown he began teaching them in their synagogue, so that they were amazed, and said, Where did he get this wisdom and these powers? Isn't this the carpenter's son? Isn't Mary his mother? Aren't James, Joseph, Simon and Judas his brothers? Aren't all his sisters here with us? Where did this man get all these things? And they took offence at him. But Jesus said to them, A prophet is not dishonoured, except in his own town and among his own kin. So he didn't do many mighty works there, because of their unbelief.

Chapter Fourteen

John the Baptist beheaded vv1—12

At that time Herod the Tetrarch heard about the fame of Jesus, and said to his servants, This must be John the Baptist! He's been raised from the dead! That's why these miraculous powers are at work in him. For Herod had arrested John, bound him and put him in jail on account of Herodias, his brother Philip's wife. Because John kept telling him, It's unlawful for you to have her. Although he wanted to put him to death, he feared the crowd, who held John to be a prophet.

But on Herod's birthday, Herodias' daughter danced in front of the gathering, and pleased Herod, so much so that he vowed under oath to give her whatever she asked. Prompted by her mother, she says, Give to me here the head of John the Baptist on a plate. And the king was saddened; but because of his oaths to his guests, he sent and had John beheaded in the jail. So his head was brought on a plate, and given to the young girl who gave it to her mother. His disciples then came and took the body and buried it, and they went and told Jesus.

Feeding five thousand vv13–21

When Jesus heard this, he left in a boat for a remote place, in private. But when the crowds heard about it, they followed him on foot from the towns. When he disembarked, he saw a large crowd and had pity on them and healed their sick. When evening came his disciples approached him, saying, This is a desolate place, and it's late. Send the crowds away to the villages, so they can buy food for themselves. But Jesus said, There's no need for them to go away—you give them something to eat. But they say, We've only five loaves here and two fish. Then he said, Bring them here to me. So he ordered the crowds to sit down on the grass, and after he took the five loaves and two fish, he looked up to heaven, said a blessing, broke the loaves and gave them to the disciples, and the disciples gave them to the crowds. And they all ate their fill. And they took up twelve baskets full of the leftovers. And those who ate were about five thousand, besides women and children.

Walking on water vv22—36

Straightaway Jesus made his disciples get into a boat and go ahead of him to the other side, while he sent the crowds away. And after dismissing the crowds, he went up to the mountainside on his own, to pray. When evening came, he was there alone. Meanwhile the boat, already far from the land, was being tossed by the waves, because the wind was against it. Shortly before dawn Jesus went out to them, walking on the sea. When the disciples saw him walking on the sea they were terrified, saying, It's a ghost! And they cried out in fear. Immediately he spoke to them, saying, Be brave! It's me! Don't be frightened! Lord, if it's you, Peter replied, order me to come to you on the water. Come on then! said Jesus. So Peter got out of the boat, and began to walk on the water towards Jesus. But when he realised the strength of the wind, he got scared, and began to sink, and shouted, Lord, save me! Straightaway Jesus reached out his hand, grabbed him, and says, What little faith you have! Why did you doubt? And as they got back into the boat the wind died. Then those in the boat worshipped him, saying, Truly, you are the Son of God.

So when they crossed over, they came to the Gennesaret region. When those there recognised Jesus they sent word to all the surrounding countryside, and they brought all their sick to him. And they begged him only to be allowed to touch the fringe of his cloak, and all who touched it were healed.

Chapter Fifteen

Breaking with tradition vv1–9

Then the Pharisees and legal experts from Jerusalem come to see Jesus, saying, Why do your disciples break with the tradition of the elders? For they don't wash their hands before they eat! And for what reason, he answered them, do you disobey God's commandment for the sake of your tradition? For God said, Honour your father and mother, and whoever dishonours them will be put to death. But you say, If someone tells his father or mother, whatever gift you would have got from me belongs to God, then there's no need to honour his father. So for the sake of your tradition you ignore God's word. Hypocrites! How well did Isaiah prophesy about you when he says, **This people honour me with their lips, but as for their heart—it's far from me. In vain they worship me, teaching human precepts, as if they were Torah.**

Impurity Defined vv 10–20

Then he called the crowd to him and said, Hear and understand. It's not what goes into a person's mouth that defiles him; but what comes out, that's what defiles him. Then the disciples came to him, and say, Do you know that when the Pharisees heard this saying they were scandalised? He replied, Every plant not planted by my heavenly Father will be uprooted. Let them be; they're blind guides. If the blind lead the blind both will fall into a ditch. Peter said to him, Explain this parable to us. Jesus said, Do you still lack understanding? Don't you see that what goes into the mouth passes through the stomach, and exits through the sewer? But what comes out of the mouth comes from the heart, and this is what defiles a person. Because out of the heart come evil thoughts, murder, adultery, sexual immorality, theft, false testimony, slander. These are what defile a person—not eating with unwashed hands

Healing through faith vv21–28

And Jesus left that area and went to the district of Tyre and Sidon. And who should come up to him, but a Canaanite woman from that region crying out, saying, Have pity on me, Lord, Son of David, my daughter is demon possessed. But he said nothing, and his disciples came and were imploring him, saying, Get rid of her, because she's shouting after us. He replied, I was only sent to the lost sheep of the house of Israel. But she came and kneeling before him says, Lord, help me! He answered, It's not right to take the children's bread and toss it to the dogs. True, Lord, she said, but even the dogs eat the crumbs that fall from the master's table. Then Jesus replied, Woman, great is your faith! As you wish—so may it be! And at that very hour her daughter was healed.

Many healed vv29–31

And Jesus went on from there, and passed along the Sea of Galilee. And he went up into the mountain and sat down there. And large crowds came to him bringing with them the lame, the blind, the crippled, the mute and many others, and they laid them down at his feet, and he healed them. The crowd were amazed when they saw the mute speaking, the crippled restored, the lame walking, and the blind seeing. And they glorified the God of Israel.

The hungry fed vv32–39

Then Jesus called his disciples to him, and said, I feel compassion for the crowd because they've been with me three days now and have nothing to eat. I can't send them away hungry in case they collapse on their way. And his disciples say to him, Where can we get enough bread to feed so many in such a remote spot? Jesus says to them, How many loaves have you got? They said, Seven and a few small fish. So he instructed the crowd to sit on the ground. And taking the seven loaves and the fish, he gave thanks and broke them and began to give them to the disciples, and the disciples to the crowds. And they all ate and were satisfied. And they collected seven baskets full of the leftovers. Those who ate numbered four thousand, not counting women and children. After sending the crowds away, he got into a boat and came to the regions of Magadan.

Chapter Sixteen

Request for a sign rejected vv1—4

The Pharisees and Sadducees came to Jesus to test him. They asked him to show them a sign from heaven. He replied saying, When evening comes you say, It's going to be fair because the sky is red; and in the morning it's going to be stormy because the sky is red and gloomy. You know how to interpret the weather, but not the signs of the times. An evil and adulterous generation wants a sign, but none will be given it except Jonah's sign. He then left them and went off.

Beware the teaching of the Pharisees and Sadducees vv5–12

The disciples arrived at the other side, but had forgotten to bring bread. Watch out, Jesus warned them, be on your guard against the yeast of the Pharisees and Sadducees. So they began to debate the matter among themselves, saying, It's because we brought no bread. When he became aware of this Jesus said to them, Why are you arguing among yourselves—men of little faith—that you have no bread? Are you still ignorant? Don't you remember the five loaves for the five thousand, and how many baskets you filled? Or the seven loaves for the four thousand, and how many baskets you collected? Why can't you grasp that I wasn't speaking to you about bread? Be on your guard against the yeast of the Pharisees and Sadducees! Then it dawned on them that he was not referring to the yeast used in bread, but about the teaching of the Pharisees and Sadducees.

Peter's confession vv13—20

Now when Jesus came to the region of Caesarea Phillippi, he asked his disciples, saying, Who do people say that the Son of Man is? They answered, Some say John the Baptist, others Elijah, and yet others Jeremiah or one of the prophets. And he says to them, But who do you say that I am? Simon Peter said, You're the Messiah, the Son of the living God! You're blessed Simon, son of John, Jesus said to him, because it wasn't flesh and blood that revealed this to you, but my Father in heaven. I tell you, You're Peter, and I'll build my church on this rock, and the gates of Hades won't overpower it. And I'll give you the keys to the kingdom of heaven, and whatever you permit on earth will already have been permitted in heaven, and whatever you allow on earth will already have been sanctioned in heaven. Then he instructed his disciples to tell nobody that he was the Messiah.

Jesus shares his fate with his disciples vv21—28

From then on, Jesus began to explain to his disciples that he must go to Jerusalem and suffer greatly at the hands of the elders, ruling priests and legal experts, and that he must be killed, and on the third day be raised. Peter took him aside and started to rebuke him saying, No Lord! Don't say that, this must never happen to you! But Jesus turned, faced him and said, Get behind me, Satan! You're a stumbling block, because you're not thinking like God but like men. Then Jesus said to his disciples, If anyone wants to follow me he must deny himself, take up his cross and follow me; for whoever wants to save his life will lose it, but anyone who loses his life for my sake will find it. For what good would it do anyone if he should gain the whole world, but forfeit his life? Or what can anyone give in exchange for his life? For the Son of Man is about to come in the glory of his Father with his angels, and then he'll repay each person according to what he's done. Truly, I tell you, there are some standing here who will not taste death until they see the Son of Man coming in his kingdom.

Chapter Seventeen

Jesus's transfiguration vv 1–13

Six days later Jesus takes Peter, James and John his brother, and leads them up a high mountain on their own. And he was transfigured in front of them: his face shone like the sun and his clothes became white as light. Suddenly Moses and Elijah appeared speaking with Jesus. Peter said to Jesus, Lord, it's great for us to be here! If you want I'll make three shelters—one each: for you, Moses and Elijah. While he was still speaking, behold a bright cloud overshadowed them, and a voice comes from out of the cloud saying, This is my son, the one I love—I'm well pleased with him—listen to what he says! When the disciples heard this they fell on their faces and were scared witless. But Jesus came to them, touched them and said, Get up, don't be afraid. When they looked up, they saw nobody except Jesus himself, alone. And as they were coming down from the mountain. Jesus instructed them saying, Tell nobody about the vision until the Son of Man has been raised from the dead. So the disciples then asked him, Why is it that the scribes say that Elijah must come first? He replied, Elijah is coming and he'll restore everything. But I'm telling you that Elijah has already come, but they didn't recognise him. Instead they treated him as they pleased. In the same way, the Son of Man is about to suffer at their hands. Then the disciples realised that he had been speaking to them about John the Baptist.

An epileptic boy healed vv14–23

And when they came to the crowd, a man came and knelt in front of Jesus and said, Lord, take pity on my son, he's an epileptic and suffers terribly. For he often falls into both fire and water. I did bring him to your disciples, but they couldn't cure him. Jesus answered, saying, Faithless and crooked generation! How long must I be with you? How long do I have to tolerate you? Bring him here to me. Jesus rebuked the demon and it came out of him, and the boy was cured instantly. Then the disciples came to Jesus privately and said, Why couldn't we cast it out? Jesus says to them, Because your faith is so little. I tell you the truth, if you've faith the size of a mustard seed you can say to this mountain, Move from here to there, and it'll move! Nothing will be impossible for you. When they were still together in Galilee Jesus said to them, The Son of Man is about to be delivered into the hands of men. They will kill him, and he will be raised on the third day. And they were deeply upset.

How to pay the Temple tax vv24–27

When they arrived at Capernaum the temple tax collectors approached Peter and said, Doesn't your teacher pay the two-drachma tax? Yes, he answers. When he went into the house Jesus spoke to Peter first, saying, What do you think, Simon, from whom do earthly kings collect tolls and taxes: from their children or from strangers? And he answered, From strangers. So the sons are exempt, said Jesus. But in case we cause offence, go to the sea and cast a hook, and take the first fish that comes up. And when you have opened its mouth, you'll find a two-drachma coin, give it to them as my tax and yours.

Chapter Eighteen

Who is the greatest in the Kingdom of heaven?
vv 1—9

At that time the disciples came to Jesus, asking,
Who's the greatest in the kingdom of heaven?
Calling to himself a child, he set it among them
and said, Really, unless you change and become
like little children, you'll never enter the kingdom
of heaven. Whoever humbles himself like this child
is the greatest in the kingdom of heaven. And
whoever welcomes a child like this in my name,
welcomes me. But should anyone cause one of
these these little ones to sin, it would be better
for him if a huge millstone were hung round his
neck and he were drowned in the depths of the
sea. Woe to the world for its temptations to sin!
Temptations are bound to come; but woe to the
person through whom they come! If your hand or
foot makes you sin, cut it off and throw it away.
It's better for you to enter in to life crippled or

lame, than to have two hands or two feet, and to be thrown into the hell of fire. And if your eye makes you sin, gouge it out. It's better to enter into life with one eye, than to have two eyes and be thrown into the hell of fire.

A lost sheep vv10–14

See that you don't despise one of these little ones. For I'm telling you their angels in heaven always see the face of my Father in heaven. What do you think? If someone owns a hundred sheep and one goes missing, won't he leave the ninety-nine on the mountains and look for the one that went astray? And if he finds it, truly I tell you, he rejoices over it more than over the ninety-nine that didn't go astray. So it's not the will of your Father in heaven that one of these little ones should perish.

Lessons in forgiveness vv15–20

If your brother sins against you, go and tell him his fault between you and him alone, and if he listens to you, you have won over your brother. But if he doesn't listen, take one or two others with you so that, **By the mouth of two or three**

witnesses every word may be confirmed. And if he ignores them, report it to the church. And if he doesn't listen even to the church, then treat him as a Gentile and tax collector. In truth, I tell you, whatever you bind on earth shall be what's already been bound in heaven; and whatever you loose on earth shall be what's already been loosed in heaven. Again I tell you, if two of you agree on earth about anything they ask, my Father in heaven will do it for them. For where two or three are gathered together in my name, there I am among them.

The unforgiving servant vv21–35

Peter then came up and said to him, Lord, how often when my brother sins against me must I forgive him? Seven times? Jesus says to him, I don't say to you seven times, but seventy times seven. Therefore the kingdom of heaven is like a king who wished to settle an account with his servants. As he began to settle it, one of them was brought to him who owed him ten thousand talents. And because he could not pay, his master ordered him to be sold, and his wife and children and all he had, so that payment could be made. The servant then fell on his knees and implores him saying, Be patient with me and

I'll pay you everything! Moved with pity, that servant's master released him and forgave him the debt. But when that same servant went out, he found one of his fellow servants who owed him a hundred denarii, and seizing him he began to choke him, saying, Pay what you owe! So his fellow servant fell down and pleaded with him, Have patience and I'll pay you. But he refused, and he went and put him in prison until he should pay the debt. His fellow servants, on seeing what had happened, were greatly distressed and they went and reported to their master all that had taken place. Then his master summoned him and said, You wicked servant! You pleaded with me and I forgave you all that debt. Shouldn't you have had mercy on your fellow servant, as I had mercy on you? In anger his master handed him over to the jailers, until he should pay all that he owed. This is what my heavenly Father will do to each of you, if you do not forgive your brother from your heart.

Chapter Nineteen

Is divorce permitted? vv 1—12

So when Jesus finished saying all this, he left Galilee and came to the Judean regions on the other side of the Jordan. Large crowds followed him and he healed them there. And some Pharisees came to him to test him, asking, Is it lawful for a husband to divorce his wife for any reason? Haven't you heard, Jesus replied, that from the beginning, **He made them male and female?** That's why, **A man will leave his father and mother and be united with his wife, and the two will become one flesh.** So they're no longer two, but one flesh. So let no one separate what God's joined together. Why then, they ask him, did Moses order that a husband give his wife a divorce certificate and send her away? Jesus answers them, Moses let you divorce your wives because of your hard hearts. This wasn't how it was in the beginning. So I tell you, whoever divorces his wife, except for sexual immorality, commits adultery. His disciples say to him, If that's what marriage is like then better not get married at all! But he answered them, Not everyone can receive this teaching, except those to whom it has been granted. For there's eunuchs who have been eunuchs from their mother's womb, and there's eunuchs who were made eunuchs by others, and still others who made themselves eunuchs for the kingdom of heaven's sake. Whoever is able to accept this—let them accept it.

Children blessed vv 13–15

Then children were brought to him so that he might lay his hands on them and pray. But the disciples scolded those who brought them. Jesus said, Let the children come to me—don't try to stop them, for to such belongs the kingdom of heaven. And after he had placed his hands on them he left.

The rich young ruler tested vv 16–27

And behold a young man came to Jesus and said, Teacher, what good deed must I do to have eternal life? He answered him, Why do you ask me about what's good? There's only one who's good. But if you want to enter into life, keep the commandments. He asks him, Which ones? Jesus said, **Don't murder, Don't commit adultery, Don't steal, Don't give false evidence, Honour your father and mother, and love your neighbour as yourself.** The young man says to him, I've kept all these! So what do I lack? Jesus said to him, If you want to be perfect, go and sell all your possessions and give to the poor, and you'll have treasure in heaven—and come, follow me! When the young man heard this he went away in sadness, because he had many possessions. Jesus said to his disciples, In truth I tell you, it's difficult for a rich person to enter the kingdom of heaven; indeed I tell you it's easier for a camel to go through a needle's eye than for a rich person to enter the kingdom of God. When they heard this the disciples were stunned, saying, Who then can be saved? Jesus looked them in the eye, and said, People can't do this—it's impossible; but with God everything's possible. Peter responded, saying to him, Look, we've left everything and followed you—what's in it for us? Jesus said to them, I tell you the truth in the new age, when the Son of Man sits on his glorious throne, you who've followed me will also sit on twelve thrones judging the twelve tribes of Israel. And everyone who has left homes, or brothers or sisters or father or mother or children or fields, for the sake of my name, will inherit eternal life. But many who are first will be last, and the last first.

Chapter Twenty

A fair wage? vv1–16

For the kingdom of heaven's like this: a vineyard owner went out in the early morning to hire workers for his vineyard. And after agreeing with the workers to pay them the standard daily rate, he sent them to his vineyard. And going out at about nine o'clock, he saw others standing idly in the market place. He said to them, Off you go as well and work in my vineyard, and I'll pay you what's right. So off they went. Again he went out about noon and then around three o'clock, and did the same thing. At about five o'clock he found others standing around and he says to them, Why are you standing around idle all day? They say to him, Because nobody hired us. He says to them, Off you go too and work in my vineyard. When evening came the vineyard owner says to his foreman, Call the workers and pay them their wages, beginning with the last and then going on to the first. So those hired about five o'clock came and each received the daily rate; but when those hired first came they expected to receive more, but they also received the same pay. When they took it they began to complain to the vineyard owner saying, This lot has only worked an hour, yet you've treated them the same as us, though we've had to withstand the scorching heat of the day! But he answered one of them and said, Friend, I'm not being unfair to you. Didn't you agree with me to work for the standard rate? Take what you've earned and be gone. Am I not permitted do what I like with my own money? Or is it that you despise my generosity? So the last will be first and the first last.

Jesus tells his disciples what will happen to him
vv17—19

As he was going up to Jerusalem, Jesus took aside the twelve, and along the way says to them, Look, we're going up to Jerusalem, and the Son of Man will be handed over to the chief priests and scribes. And they'll condemn him to death, and hand him over to the Gentiles to be mocked, flogged, and crucified, and on the third day he will be raised up.

Jesus speaks to a mother vv20–28

Then the mother of Zebedee approached Jesus and kneeling down asks him for something. He said to her, What do you want? Let one of these two sons of mine, she says, sit at your right hand and the other on your left in your kingdom. Jesus replied, Neither of you know what you're asking. Can any of you drink the cup I'm going to drink? We can, they reply. Jesus says to them, You will indeed drink from my cup, but as for sitting on my right hand and on my left, it's not up to me, but it's for those for whom it's been prepared by my Father. When the ten heard this they became angry with the two brothers. But Jesus called them and said, You know that the rulers of the Gentiles lord it over them, and their rulers in turn exercise authority over them; but it'll not be like that among you. Whoever wants to be great among you must become your servant, and whoever wants to be first among you must be your slave. For the Son of Man didn't come to be served but to serve, and to give his life as a ransom for many.

Two blind men vv29–34

As they were leaving Jericho, a large crowd followed him. And sitting by the roadside were two blind men. When they heard that Jesus was passing by, they cried out, saying, Pity us Lord, Son of David! The crowd reproved them and told them to shut up, but they shouted out all the louder, Pity us Lord, Son of David! Jesus stopped and called them, saying, What do you want me to do for you? Let our eyes be opened, Lord, they answer. Moved with compassion, Jesus touched their eyes, and straightaway they regained their sight, and followed him.

Chapter Twenty-One

The coming king vv 1–11

Now as they approached Jerusalem and came to Bethphage, at the Mount of Olives, Jesus sent two disciples, saying to them, Go to the village ahead of you, and straightaway you'll see a donkey tied, and a colt with her. Untie them and bring them to me. And if anybody says anything to you, say, The Lord needs them; then he'll send them at once. This happened to fulfill what was spoken through the prophet, saying, **Tell the daughter of Zion, Behold, your king comes to you, humble, mounted on a donkey, and on a colt, the foal of a donkey.** So the disciples went and did as Jesus told them. They brought the donkey and colt, put their cloaks on them, and he sat on them. A very large crowd spread their cloaks on the road, while others cut down branches from the trees, and were spreading them on the road. The crowds moving ahead of him, and those following, were shouting, **Hosanna** to the Son of David! ***Blessed is the one who comes in the name of the Lord! Hosanna*** in the highest! And when he entered Jerusalem the entire city was in turmoil, saying, Who's this? The crowds kept repeating, This is the prophet Jesus, from Nazareth in Galilee.

Jesus in the temple vv12—17

And Jesus went into the temple and drove out all those selling and buying there. He overturned the tables of the moneychangers and the seats of those selling doves. It's written, he says to them, ***My house shall be called a house of prayer,*** but you've made it a den for thieves. The blind and the crippled came to him in the temple, and he healed them. But when the chief priests and the scribes saw the marvelous works he performed, and the children shouting in the temple, Hosanna to the Son of David! they were angry and they said to him, Can you hear what they're saying? Yes, Jesus says to them, and have you never read, ***Out of the mouths of infants and nursing babies you have drawn out praise***? So he left them and went out of the city, and came to Bethphage where he spent the night.

The barren fig tree vv18–22

In the early morning, as he was returning to the city, Jesus felt hungry, and when he saw a fig tree at the roadside he went over to it but found nothing on it except leaves. And he says to it, Nevermore bear fruit! At once the tree withered. When the disciples saw this they were amazed, saying, How did the fig tree wither so quickly? Jesus answered them, The truth is, if you've faith and don't doubt, not only will you be able to do what was done to the fig tree, you'll be able to say to this mountain, Up! Get yourself into the sea! and it will happen. And whatever you ask in prayer, you'll receive if you believe.

Questioning the authority of Jesus vv23—27

When he entered the temple, the ruling priests and the elders approached him as he was teaching. By what authority are you doing these things? they asked. Who gave you this authority? Jesus answered them, saying, I'll ask you one question as well, and if you answer me, then I'll tell you by what authority I do these things. John's baptism: where did it come from; heaven or men? They began debating among themselves, If we say, From heaven, he'll say to us, Then why didn't you believe him? But if we say, From men, we have the crowd to fear, for all hold John to be a prophet. We don't know, they said to Jesus. He also said to them, Neither will I tell you by what authority I'm doing these things.

Two sons vv28—32

What do you think? A certain man had two sons. And when he approached the first he said, Come on, boy, go and work in the vineyard today. He answered, No, I won't. But later he changed his mind and went. When he approached the other he said the same. He answered, I will, sir. But he didn't go. Which of the two did as his Father wished? They say, The first. The truth is, says Jesus, tax collectors and prostitutes are entering the kingdom of God ahead of you! For John came to show you the way of righteousness, but you didn't believe him—however tax collectors and prostitutes did believe him. And even though you saw it, you didn't afterwards change your minds and believe him.

Sinful tenants vv33–46

Here's another parable. A landowner planted a vineyard, built a fence around it, dug a winepress, and built a watchtower. Then he rented it to winegrowers and went away. Come harvest, he sent his servants to the winegrowers to collect his share of the crop. But the winegrowers seized the servants, and beat one, killed another and stoned a third. Then he sent other servants, more this time, and they did the same to them. Finally, he sent his son, saying, They'll respect my son, surely. But when the winegrowers saw the son they said to each other, This is the heir— come on, let's kill him and we'll have his inheritance. So they seized him, threw him out of the vineyard and killed him. So what'll the owner of the vineyard do to those tenants when he comes back? They say to him, He'll bring those wretches to a gruesome end, and give the vineyard to other tenants, who'll give him his share of the crop at harvest time. Jesus says to them, haven't you ever read the scriptures? **The stone the builders rejected has become the cornerstone. This is the Lord's doing and is marvelous in** our sight. Therefore I tell you, the kingdom of God will be taken from you and given to those who produce its fruit. Anyone who falls on this stone will be broken to pieces; and anyone on whom it falls will be crushed.

When the chief priests and the Pharisees heard his parables, they realized that he was speaking about them. Although they wanted to arrest him, they feared the mob because they believed that he was a prophet.

Chapter Twenty-Two

Guests at a wedding vv 1–14

So again Jesus spoke to them in parables, saying, The kingdom of heaven is like a king who prepared a wedding banquet for his son, and sent out his servants to summon those invited to the feast. But they wouldn't come. So he sent different servants, saying, Tell those invited, Look, I've prepared my banquet, my oxen and fattened calves have been slaughtered, and it's all ready. Come to the wedding feast! But they took no notice: one went off to his farm, another to his business, while the rest seized his servants and treated them shamefully and killed them. The king was furious, and sent his soldiers and destroyed those murderers, and burned their city. Then he says to his servants, The wedding banquet is ready, but those invited were unworthy. So head out on to the roads, and invite anyone you find to come to the banquet. The servants went out and brought in everyone they could find, both evil and good. So the wedding hall was packed with guests. When the king came in to have a good look at the guests, he noticed there a man not wearing a wedding outfit, so he says to him, Friend, how did you get in without a wedding outfit? The man was speechless. Then the king said to his staff, Tie him up, hand and foot, and throw him into outer darkness, where there'll be wailing and gnashing of teeth. For many are called, but few chosen.

Taxes for Caesar vv15–22

Then the Pharisees went and plotted to trap him in his speech. So they send their own followers to him along with the Herodians, saying, Teacher, we know that you've integrity and teach God's way truthfully and defer to nobody, and you're not swayed by appearances. So tell us, what's your opinion? Is it right to pay tax to Caesar, yes or no? But Jesus saw through their evil purpose. He said, Why are you testing me, you hypocrites? Show me the coin used for the tax. So they brought a denarius to him. He says to them, Whose image and inscription is this? Caesar's, they reply. Then give to Caesar what's Caesar's, and to God what belongs to God. When they heard this they were stunned, so they left him and went away.

Marriage and resurrection vv23–33

That same day Sadducees (who say that there is no resurrection) came to him and said, Teacher, Moses said that, **If a man dies with no children, his brother must marry his widow and raise children for his brother**. So let's say there were seven brothers. The first one married her and died, and since he'd no children, he left his widow to his brother. Then the second died, the third, and so on, to the seventh. Eventually, the woman died as well. In the resurrection then, whose wife will she be, since they'd all been married to her? Jesus answered, You err, because you don't know the scriptures nor God's power, because in the resurrection they won't marry nor be given in marriage—they'll be like the angels in heaven. And as far as the resurrection of the dead is concerned, haven't you read what God said, **I am the God of Abraham, Isaac and Jacob**? He's not the God of the dead, but of the living! And when the crowd heard this, they were taken aback at his teaching.

The greatest commandment vv34–40

When the Pharisees heard that Jesus had silenced the Sadducees, they met together, and one of them, a legal expert, asked him a question to test him. Teacher, which is the greatest commandment in the law? He said to him, **You shall love the Lord your God with all your heart, and with all your soul and with all your mind**. This is the first and greatest commandment. And the second's just like it, **You shall love your neighbour as yourself**. Everything in the law and the prophets hinge on these two commandments.

Whose son is the Messiah? vv41—46

While the Pharisees were gathered together, Jesus asked them, saying, What do you think of the Messiah? Whose son is he? David's, they reply. He says to them, Why then does David, speaking by the Spirit, call him Lord, saying, **The Lord said to my Lord, Sit on my right, until I put your enemies under your feet?** If David calls him Lord, how can he be his son? Nobody said a word to him in reply. And from then on, no one dared to ask him any more questions.

Chapter Twenty-Three

Hypocrisy and a lament over Jerusalem vv1–39

Then Jesus spoke to the crowds and to his disciples, saying, The scribes and the Pharisees sit on Moses' seat. So you must do, and continue to pay heed to, whatever they tell you. But don't do what they do, for they preach but don't practice. They tie up heavy and burdensome loads and put them on others' shoulders, while being unwilling to lift a finger to move them. They do everything to be seen by others. They enlarge their phylacteries and lengthen the tassels on their clothing. They love the place of honour at banquets and the best seat in the synagogue, and being saluted in the market place, and to be called, Rabbi, by others. But you shouldn't be called, Rabbi, because you've one teacher, and you are all brothers. And don't call anyone on earth, Father, for you've one Father who's in heaven. On no account either should you be called, Teacher, because the Messiah is your one and only teacher. And the greatest among you will be your servant. Whoever exalts himself will be humbled, and whoever humbles himself will be exalted. But woe to you scribes and Pharisees—hypocrites! You shut the door of the kingdom of heaven in people's faces. You don't go in yourselves, and neither do you allow those who are entering to go in. Woe to you scribes and Pharisees, hypocrites! You travel over land and sea to make a single convert, but when he becomes one you make him twice as much a child of hell as yourselves. Woe to you, blind guides! You say if anyone swears by the temple it means nothing, but if anyone swears by the gold that's in the temple he's oath bound. Blind fools! For what's more important, the gold or the temple, which sanctifies the gold? You also say if anyone swears by the altar that means nothing, but if anyone swears by the gift on the altar he's oath bound. Blind men! For what's more important, the gift or the altar that makes the gift sacred? So anyone who swears by the altar swears not only by it, but also by everything on it. And anyone who swears by the temple, swears by it and by the one who dwells there. And anyone who swears by heaven, swears by God's throne and by the one who sits on it. Woe to you, scribes and Pharisees— hypocrites! You tithe mint and dill and cumin, but have neglected the greater matters of the law—justice, mercy, and faithfulness. You should have done these things without neglecting the others. Blind guides! You strain out a gnat but swallow a camel! Woe to you, scribes and Pharisees—hypocrites! You clean the cup and dish on the outside, but inside they are full of greed and self-indulgence. You blind Pharisee! Clean the inside of the cup and dish first, so that the outside may be clean as well. Woe to you, scribes and Pharisees—hypocrites! You are like whitewashed tombs that look exquisite on the outside, but inside are full of dead men's bones and everything filthy. So on the outside you appear righteous to people, but on the inside you are full of hypocrisy and lawlessness. Woe to you, scribes and Pharisees! You build the tombs of the prophets and adorn the monuments of the righteous and claim, If we'd lived in our fathers' time we wouldn't have joined them in shedding the blood of the prophets. So then you incriminate yourselves, because you are the descendants of those who murdered the prophets! Carry on and finish what your ancestors started! You snakes, children of vipers! How will you avoid the judgment of hell? Therefore, behold, I'm sending you prophets, wise people and scribes. You will kill and crucify some, others you will flog in your synagogue and chase them from town to town, so that you will be responsible for all the righteous blood being shed on earth, from the blood of righteous Abel to the blood of Zechariah, Berekiah's son, that you murdered between the temple and the altar. I'm telling you bluntly, all this will befall this generation. Jerusalem, Jerusalem, that kills the prophets and stones those sent to her! How often have I longed to gather together your children, as a hen gathers her young chickens under her wings, but you were unwilling. See, your house is left desolate! I'm telling you, you won't see me from now on until you say: **Blessed is he who comes in the Lord's name.**

Chapter Twenty-Four

The destruction of the temple and the end of the age vv1—51

Then Jesus left the temple and was walking away. His disciples came to him to point out the temple buildings. He said to them, You see all these, don't you? I tell you the truth: not a single stone will be left on another. All will be thrown down. When Jesus was sitting on the Mount of Olives his disciples approached him privately, saying, Tell us, when will all these things happen, and what'll be the sign of your coming and of the end of the age? Jesus answered them, Take care no one misleads you. Many will come using my name and saying, I'm the Messiah, and will mislead many. You'll hear about wars and rumours of wars, but don't panic—this must happen—but the end is not yet. Nation will be raised against nation and kingdom against kingdom. There'll be famines and earthquakes in various places. All these things are just the beginning of the birth pangs. Then they'll hand you over to be persecuted and they'll kill you, and you will be hated by all nations because of me. Then many will fall away and betray and hate one another. And many false prophets will be raised up and lead many astray. Because lawlessness will increase, the love of many will grow cold. But whoever stands fast to the end will be saved. And then this gospel of the kingdom will be proclaimed to the whole world as a testimony to all nations, and then the end will come. So whenever you see **the abomination that causes desolation,** standing in the holy place (as the prophet Daniel foretold— let the reader understand), then those in Judea should flee to the mountains. No one on the housetop should go down to take anything out of the house. Whoever happens to be in the fields shouldn't return to get his cloak. And there'll be woe for pregnant women and nursing mothers at that time. Pray that your escape won't be in winter or on the sabbath. For there'll be great distress such as has not been experienced since the world's creation, and such as will never be experienced again. No one would survive if those days weren't shortened, but they will be shortened; for the sake of the chosen ones. Then if anyone says to you, Look, here's the Messiah! Or, There he is! Don't believe them. Because false messiahs and false prophets will be raised up, and they'll perform great signs and wonders to lead astray, if that were possible, even the elect. So watch out! I've told you in advance! If they say to you, He's out there in the wilderness! Don't go out, or, He's here in the inner rooms, don't believe it. For just as lightning flashes in the east and is visible as far as the west, so will be the Son of Man's coming. For vultures will gather wherever there's a corpse. Immediately after the tribulation of those days, the sun will be darkened and the moon will not give its light, and the stars will be falling from heaven and the powers of the heavens will be shaken. And then sign of the Son of Man will appear in heaven and all the earth's tribes will mourn, and they'll see the Son of Man coming on the clouds of heaven with power and great glory. And he'll send his angels with a loud trumpet call, and they'll gather his chosen ones from the four winds, from one end of heaven to the other. Learn the lesson of the fig tree; as soon as its branch becomes tender and it sprouts its leaves, you know summer's on its way. In the same way, when you see all these things, you know he's near, at the gates. Truly I tell you, this generation won't pass away until all these things happen. Heaven and earth will pass away, but my words won't pass away. No one knows that day and hour—not even the angels in heaven or the Son, but only the Father. The coming of the Son of Man will be just like the days of Noah. For as people were eating and drinking, marrying and giving in marriage, right up until the time Noah entered the ark, they were unaware, until the flood came and swept everyone away. So will be the coming of the Son of Man. Two men will be in a field, one will be taken and the other left. Two women will be grinding at the mill, one will be taken, the other left. So be vigilant, because you don't know when your Lord is coming. But know this, if the householder had known what part of the night the thief was coming, he would've stayed awake and wouldn't have allowed his house to be broken into. So be ready, because the Son of Man is coming when you least expect him. Who then is the loyal and wise servant that his master has put in charge of his household, to feed them at the right time? Happy will be the servant whose master will find him so doing when he returns home. In truth I tell you, he'll put him in charge of all his possessions. But if in the case of a wicked servant, who says to himself, My master's held up, so he starts to assault his fellow servants and eats and drinks with drunkards, the master will come unexpectedly, and cut him in two and put him with the hypocrites, where there'll be weeping and gnashing of teeth.

Chapter Twenty-Five

Virgins wise and otherwise vv 1—13

So the kingdom of heaven will be like ten virgins who took their lamps and went out to meet the bridegroom. Five were stupid and five sensible. Because when the stupid ones took their lamps they didn't take any oil with them; but the wise ones took flasks of oil with their lamps. As the bridegroom was delayed, they all became drowsy. But at midnight there was a cry, Here's the bridegroom! Come out to meet him! The virgins got up and prepared their lamps. The stupid ones said to the sensible ones, Give us some of your oil, because our lamps are going out. The sensible ones replied, saying, We don't have enough for us and for you. Go to the suppliers and buy your own. And while they were going to buy it, the bridegroom came. Those who were ready went with him to the marriage feast; then the door was locked. Later the other virgins come saying, Lord, Lord open to us! He answered, Truly, I tell you, I don't know you. Watch therefore, because you don't know the day or the hour.

Talents used and wasted vv14–30

It'll be like this: a man was setting out on a journey, and summoned his servants and entrusted his property to them. He gave five talents to one, to another two, and to another one, according to his ability. And he departed. The one with five talents immediately traded with them, and made five more. Similarly, the man with two talents made two more. But he who had received the one talent went off, dug a hole in the ground and hid his master's money. After a long time the master of those servants comes and settles accounts with them. The one with five talents came up bringing five more, saying. Master you gave me five talents, I've made five more. His master said to him, Well done! You're a good and loyal servant. You've been loyal over a little, so I'll put you in charge of more. Enter into your master's joy. Then the one with two talents came up and said, Master you gave me two talents, look I've made two more. His master said to him, Well done! You're a good and loyal servant. You've been loyal over a little, so I'll put you in charge of more. Enter into your Master's joy. But the one who had received the one talent came forward, and said, Lord, I knew you were a harsh man, reaping where you didn't sow and harvesting where you hadn't scattered any seed. So I was afraid and I went and hid your talent in the ground. Here's what's yours, take it. But his master answered him, You wicked and lazy servant! You know I reap where I haven't sown, and harvest where I haven't scattered seed. So you should've invested my money with the bankers, so that when I returned I would get back what was mine with interest. Take the talent from him, and give it to the one with ten talents. So to everyone who has, more will be given, and they'll have abundance. But as for the one who has nothing, even what he has will be taken away from him. And cast out the worthless servant too into outer darkness, where there'll be weeping and grinding of teeth.

The Day of Judgment vv31—46

Whenever the Son of Man comes in his glory, together with all the angels, he will sit on his glorious throne. All the nations will be gathered before him, and he will separate them from each other, as a shepherd separates the sheep from the goats. And he will place the sheep on his right, and the goats on the left. Then the king will say to those on his right, Come, you who are blessed by my Father, receive the kingdom prepared for you from the creation of the world. For I was hungry and you fed me, thirsty and you gave me drink, a stranger and you welcomed me, naked and you dressed me, sick and you visited me, in prison and you came to me. Then the righteous will answer saying, Lord, when did we see you hungry and feed you, or thirsty and give you drink? And when did we see you a stranger and welcome you, or naked and clothe you? And when did we see you sick, or in prison and visit you? And the king will say, truly I tell you, as you did it to the least of my brothers, you did it to me. Then he'll say to those on his left, Away from me, you cursed, into the eternal fire prepared for the devil and his angels! For I was hungry and you didn't feed me, thirsty and you didn't give me a drink, I was a stranger and you didn't welcome me, naked and you didn't clothe me, sick and in prison and you didn't visit me. Then they'll also answer saying, Lord, when did we see you hungry or thirsty, or a stranger or naked, or sick or in prison, and didn't help you? Then he'll answer them saying, Truly I tell you, inasmuch as you didn't do it to the least of these my brothers, you didn't do it to me. So these will go to eternal punishment, but the righteous into eternal life.

Chapter Twenty-Six

The plot to kill Jesus vv 1–5

When Jesus had finished saying all this, he said to his disciples, You're aware that it will be Passover in two days, and the Son of Man will be handed over to be crucified. Then the chief priests and the elders of the people got together in the lodgings of Caiaphas, the high priest, and plotted together to arrest Jesus secretly and kill him. But they were saying, Not during the feast, or there'll be uproar among the people.

Anointing for burial vv6–13

Now when Jesus was at Bethany at the home of Simon the leper, a woman came up to him with an alabaster flask of expensive ointment, and poured it on his head as he reclined at supper. And when his disciples saw it, they were indignant, saying, What a waste! This could've been sold and the proceeds given to the poor. But Jesus, aware of this, said to them, Why give this woman grief? She's done something beautiful to me. You've got the poor with you always, but you won't always have me. By pouring this ointment on me she's prepared my body for burial. In truth, I tell you, wherever this gospel's proclaimed throughout the world, what she's done will also be told in memory of her.

Judas betrays Jesus vv14–25

Judas Iscariot, one of the twelve, went to the chief priests and said, What'll you give me if I hand him over to you? They paid him thirty pieces of silver. From then on he began to look for an opportunity to betray him. So on the first day of Unleavened Bread the disciples came to Jesus, saying, Where do you want us to prepare the Passover for you to eat? He said, Go into the city, to you know who, and say to him, The teacher says, My time's come; I'll keep the Passover at your house with my disciples. The disciples did as Jesus instructed them, and prepared the Passover. Come evening, he was sitting at table with the twelve, and as they were eating, he said, Truly, I tell you, one of you is going to betray me. They were devastated, and began to say in turn, Surely not me, Lord, is it? He answered, It's the one who dipped his hand in the dish with me—he's the one. The Son of Man goes, as it's written about him—but woe to that man by whom the Son of Man is betrayed! Better he'd not been born. Then Judas (who would betray him) said to him, Surely it's not me is it, Rabbi? You said it, Jesus replies.

The Lord's supper vv26–29

Now while they were eating, Jesus took bread and after blessing it, broke it and gave it to his disciples, saying, Take, eat, this is my body. And after taking a cup, he gave thanks, and gave it to them, saying, Drink it, all of you, for this is my blood of the covenant, poured out for many for the forgiveness of sins. I tell you, I'm not going to drink this fruit of the vine until the time I'll drink it again with you in my Father's kingdom. So when they had sung a hymn, they went to the Mount of Olives.

Jesus predicts Peter's denial vv31–35

Then Jesus says to them, You'll all desert me tonight, for it's written, **I will strike the shepherd, and the flock of sheep will be scattered.** But after I'm raised, I'll go ahead of you to Galilee. Peter said him, Even if everybody else deserts you, I won't. Jesus said to him, Listen, I'll tell you, this very night, before the rooster crows, you'll deny me three times. Peter says to him, Even if I have to die with you, I won't deny you! And all the other disciples said the same.

Jesus prays in the garden vv36—46

Then Jesus goes with them to a place known as Gethsemane, and he says to his disciples, Sit here while I go and pray over there. He took Peter and the two sons of Zebedee, and became grief-stricken and distressed. Then he says to them, My sorrow is deathly; stay here and watch with me. He went a little further and fell on his face, praying and saying, My Father, if possible, take this cup from me; nevertheless, not as I will—but as you will. So he returns to the disciples and finds them sleeping, and says to Peter, Couldn't you all watch an hour with me? Watch and pray, so that you don't enter into temptation. The spirit's willing, but the flesh is weak. He went away a second time and prayed, saying, My Father, if this cup can't pass unless I drink it, your will be done. He returned again and found them sleeping, because their eyes were heavy. So he left them and he went off and prayed for the third time, using the same words. Then he comes back to the disciples and says to them, Still sleeping and resting? Behold, the hour has come! The Son of Man is delivered into the hands of sinners. Up—let's go! My betrayer's close by.

The arrest of Jesus vv47–56

As he was speaking, behold, Judas, one of the twelve, came with a large crowd with swords and clubs. They were sent from the chief priests and elders of the people. Now the betrayer had given them a signal, Whoever I kiss—he's the one—take him! Straightway he came up to Jesus, and said, Greetings, Rabbi! And he kissed him. Jesus said to him, Friend, Do what you've come for. Then they came, laid hands on Jesus and seized him. Just then, one of those with Jesus, reached out his hand, drew his sword and struck a servant of the high priest, and cut off his ear. Then Jesus says to him, Put your sword back into its sheath! For all who take up the sword will perish by the sword. Don't you think I can't appeal to my Father, and immediately he'll send me more than twelve legions of angels? But how, then, should the scriptures be fulfilled, that this is how it must be? At that moment Jesus said to the crowds, Have you come out with swords and clubs to arrest me, as if I was a robber? I used to sit teaching in the temple day after day, and you never arrested me. But all this has happened, so that what the prophets wrote might be fulfilled. Then all the disciples left him and ran away.

Jesus examined before Caiaphas vv57–68

And those who had seized Jesus led him to Caiaphas, the high priest, where the scribes and elders had gathered. And Peter was following him at a distance, as far as the courtyard of the high priest. He went inside, and sat with the guards to see what would happen. Now the chief priests and the whole council were looking for false testimony against Jesus, so that they might put him to death. But they found none, although many false witnesses came forward. Eventually, two showed up and said, This fellow was saying I can destroy God's temple and rebuild it in three days. And the high priest got up, and said, Have you no answer? What are these men testifying against you? But Jesus was silent. Then the high priest said to him, I put you on oath, by the living God, tell us are you the Messiah, the Son of God? Jesus says to him, You said it. But I tell you, from now on you'll see **the Son of Man sitting on the right hand of power and coming on the clouds of heaven.** At this, the high priest ripped his clothes, and said, He's blasphemed, what other witnesses do we need?—now you've heard the blasphemy! What's your verdict? He deserves death, they answered. Then they spat in his face and struck him. Some slapped him, saying, Prophesy to us, Messiah, who struck you?

Peter denies Jesus vv69–75

Now Peter was sitting outside in the courtyard. And a servant girl came up to him, and says, You were with that Jesus, the Galilean, weren't you? But he denied it before everyone, saying, I've no idea what you're talking about. And when he went out into the porch another servant girl saw him, and says to those who were there, This one was with Jesus from Nazareth. And again he denied it with an oath, I don't know the man! After a little while the bystanders came up and said to Peter, For sure you're one of them, because your accent betrays you. Then he began to curse and swear an oath saying, I don't know the man! Immediately the rooster crowed. Then Peter remembered what Jesus had said, Before the rooster crows you'll deny me three times. And he went out and wept bitterly.

Chapter Twenty-Seven

Jesus sent to Pilate vv1–2

When morning came, the chief priests and elders of the people plotted against Jesus, to put him to death. And they bound and led him away, and handed him over to Pilate the governor.

Death of Judas vv3–10

Then when Judas, his betrayer, saw that Jesus was condemned, he was afflicted with remorse, and returned the thirty pieces of silver to the chief priests and the elders, saying, I've sinned by betraying innocent blood. They said, What's that got to do with us? You sort it out. So he flung the money into the temple sanctuary and left, then went off and hanged himself. But when the chief priests took the money, they said, We can't put it into the treasury because it's blood money. So after deliberating, they bought the potter's field with the money, as a burial ground for strangers. That's why that field is called, Field of Blood, to this day. Then what Jeremiah the prophet said was fulfilled, **And they took the thirty pieces of silver, the value of him set by some of the children of Israel. And they used them to buy the potter's field, as the Lord ordered me.**

Jesus before Pilate vv11–14

So Jesus was stood before the governor, and the governor asked him, Are you the King of the Jews? Jesus said, You say this. But when accused by the chief priests and the elders, he said nothing. Then Pilate says to him, Don't you hear how many charges they're bringing against you? But he did not answer him even a single word, so that the governor was greatly taken aback.

Jesus or Barabbas? vv15–23

Now it had been the custom at the feast for the governor to release to the crowd any prisoner they wanted. And they had, at that time, a notorious prisoner called Barabbas. So when they had gathered, Pilate said to them, Who do you want me to release for you: Barabbas or Jesus, called Messiah? For he knew that they had handed him over out of jealousy. And while he was sitting on the judgement seat his wife sent word to him, Don't have anything to do with that just man, because I've suffered a lot dreaming about him today. Then the chief priests and the elders persuaded the crowd that they should plead for Barabbas, and that Jesus should be destroyed. So the governor said to them again, Which of the two do you want me to release for you? And they said, Barabbas! Pilate then says to them, So what do you want me to do with Jesus, called Messiah? All of them say, Let him be crucified! And he replied, Why? What evil has he done? But they started to shout all the more, Let him be crucified!

Pilate washes his hands of Jesus vv24–26

So when Pilate realised that he was not getting anywhere, and that a riot might start, he took water and washed his hands in front of the crowd, saying, I'm innocent of this man's blood—deal with it yourselves. And all the people responded, Let his blood be upon us and upon our children!

So he released Barabbas for them and had Jesus flogged; then he handed him over to be crucified.

The soldiers mock Jesus vv27–31

Then the soldiers of the governor took Jesus into the governor's headquarters, and they mustered the entire battalion before him. And they stripped him and put a scarlet robe on him. And they twisted together a crown of thorns and put it on his head, and put a reed in his right hand, and kneeling before him they mocked him, saying, Hail! King of the Jews! And they spat on him, and took the reed and struck him on the head. And when they had mocked him they stripped him of the robe, and put his own clothes on him, and led him away to crucify him.

The crucifixion of Jesus the Messiah vv32–44

And as they went out, they found a man called Simon, from Cyrene, whom they forced to carry his cross. And when they came to a place called Golgotha (which means, the Place of a Skull), they gave him wine mixed with gall to drink, but when he tasted it, he refused to swallow it. And after they had crucified him, they throw dice to divide his clothes between them. Then they sit down, and were guarding him there. And they put the charge above his head, which read, This is Jesus, the King of the Jews. Then they crucify two robbers with him, one on the right and the other on the left. And passers by were blaspheming him, wagging their heads, saying, You who'd destroy the temple and rebuild it in three days—save yourself! If you're the Son of God, come down from the cross! The chief priests with the scribes and the elders also joined in, and were mocking him, saying, He saved others, but can't save himself! If he's the King of Israel, let him come down from the cross now, and we'll believe him. He trusts in God—let him rescue him now—if he wants to. For he said, I'm the Son of God. And the robbers crucified with him were also cursing him in the same way.

The death of Jesus Messiah vv45–56

Now there was darkness over all the earth, from noon until three o'clock. And about three o'clock, Jesus loudly cried out, *Eli, Eli, lema sabachthani?* That is, **My God, my God, why have you abandoned me?** One of the bystanders, when he heard this, kept saying,

He's calling Elijah! And someone immediately ran and took a sponge and filled it with sour wine, and put it on a reed, and gave it to him to drink. But others were saying, Wait! Let's see if Elijah comes to save him. And again, Jesus cried out loudly, and gave up his spirit. And behold, the temple curtain was rent in two, from the top to the bottom. And the earth trembled, and the rocks were split. The tombs were opened, and many bodies of holy people who had died, were raised, they came out of the tombs after his resurrection, and went into the holy city and appeared to many. Then the centurion, and those who were with him guarding Jesus, saw the earthquake and what had happened. They were terrified, saying, This really was God's Son! There also were many women there, watching from a distance. They had followed him from Galilee, serving him. Among them were Mary Magdalene, and Mary, the mother of James and Joseph, and the mother of the sons of Zebedee.

The burial of Jesus Messiah vv57–61

When evening came, Joseph, a rich man from Arimathea, who had also become a disciple of Jesus, came to Pilate and asked for Jesus's body. So Pilate ordered it to be given to him. And Joseph took the body and wrapped it in a clean linen shroud, and laid it in his own new tomb, that he had cut out of the rock. And he rolled a great stone to the entrance of the tomb, and went away. Mary Magdalene and the other Mary were there, sitting opposite the tomb.

Guarding the tomb vv62–66

The next day, that is, after the day of Preparation, the chief priests and the Pharisees assembled before Pilate saying, Sir, we remember what that deceiver said while he was still alive, After three days I will rise. So order that the tomb be made secure, until the third day, in case his disciples come and steal him and tell the people that he has risen from the dead. In this case, the last deception would be worse than the first. Then Pilate said to them, You have a detachment of soldiers, Go and make it as secure as you can. So they went and secured the tomb by sealing the stone and placing a guard.

Chapter Twenty-Eight

The resurrection of Jesus the Messiah vv1–10

After the Sabbath, at dawn, Mary Magdalene and the other Mary, went to see the tomb. And behold, there was a mighty earthquake, because an angel of the Lord had come down from heaven and rolled back the stone, and was sitting on it. His appearance was like lightning, and his clothing white as snow. For fear of him, the guards trembled and were as dead men. But the angel answered and said to the women, Don't be afraid! I know you're looking for Jesus, who's been crucified. He's not here! He's risen, just as he said. Come, see the place where he lay. Then hurry and tell his disciples that he's risen from the dead, and behold, he's going ahead of you to Galilee—you'll see him there. See, I've told you. So they fled the tomb in fear and great joy, and ran to tell his disciples. And behold, Jesus met them and said, Good morning! And they came up and grabbed hold of his feet and worshipped him. Then Jesus says to them, Don't be afraid! Go and tell my brothers to go to Galilee, and there they'll see me.

The guards report to the chief priests vv11–15

As they were on their way, behold some guards went and told the chief priests everything that had happened. And when they had met and conferred with the elders, they gave a sufficient sum of money to the soldiers, saying, Tell the people, His disciples came and stole him while we were asleep. And if the governor hears of it, we'll reassure him and keep you out of trouble. So they took the money and did as they were instructed, and this story has been spread among the Jews to this day.

Make disciples of all nations vv16–20

So the disciples went to Galilee, to the mountain where Jesus had directed them. And when they saw him they worshipped him, but some were hesitant. And Jesus came and spoke to them, saying, All authority in heaven and on earth has been given to me. Go then and make disciples of all nations, baptizing them in the name of the Father and of the Son and of the Holy Spirit, teaching them to observe all that I have commanded you. And behold, I am always with you—to the very end of the age!

Amen.